iTHRIVE

An International Student's Guide to ~~Surviving~~ Thriving in the U.S.

Lei Wang, Ph.D.

Book Production Company: Kaleidoscope Vibrations, LLC

Editors: Katherine Kolios, Nelson O. O. Zounlomè, Ph.D.

Formatter: Caroline Rinaldy

Cover Image: Stella Ko, Ph.D.

Publisher: LTB Collective Books

For more information, email: books@LiberateTheBlock.com or visit www.iTHRIVEbook.com

ISBN: 978-1-953720-03-0

About the Author

Lei Wang, Ph.D. is a licensed psychologist and tenure-track Assistant Professor. She earned her doctorate in counseling psychology with a minor in health behavior from Indiana University Bloomington in 2019.

Dr. Wang's journey as an international student first began in 1995, when she attended kindergarten and first grade in Texas (her mother was getting a master's degree in education). The journey resumed in 2011 when she attended the University of Missouri to pursue her master's in counseling psychology. Her positive experiences with research, and her interest in me-search (research related to one's own experiences), inspired her to deepen her work with Asian international and Asian American college students. She later broadened her scope to include participants from historically marginalized communities (e.g., students of color, first-generation college students).

Throughout Dr. Wang's academic journey, she received formal and informal mentorship from those who came before her. To pay it forward, Dr. Wang hopes to use this book to mentor current international students and prospective students who are interested in studying in the U.S. In writing this book, Dr. Wang envisioned a resource beyond the sparse blogs and pamphlets that individual schools developed. She sought to create a comprehensive and easily accessible compendium of existing resources, but also to encourage international students to take a hands-on approach: to research, find out what is available to them, and make the best of these resources.

While there are many resources on how to prepare for standardized tests, English proficiency tests, and university/college applications, there are few resources for international students already in the U.S. This guide emphasizes how to not only survive but thrive in the U.S.

Foreword

Dear You,

Thank you for picking up this book!

Whether you are considering studying in the U.S., have already been accepted to a school (congratulations!), or are currently in the U.S., this guide is for you.

When people ask me how I decided to study in the U.S., my answer is: it was planned happenstance (a term used in career psychology that means you prepare for a potential future opportunity, but you won't know what the opportunity is until you encounter it). I am appreciative to my parents for providing me an optimal environment so I could acquire and maintain my English skills when I was growing up. I had the privilege to accompany my mother to the States as she pursued her master's degree in education while I attended kindergarten and first grade. I was also homeschooled for four years before I started attending public school in sixth grade. The movie Mean Girls came out around that time and it is still one of my favorite movies because the experiences of Lindsay Lohan's character resonated with me as someone who entered public school for the first time.

As students in Taiwanese public schools, my peers and I were expected to help clean our learning environment. From elementary to high school, cleaning was a daily chore and I was assigned to clean classrooms, restrooms, etc. In college, I was only expected to help clean once a semester. In my sophomore year, I chose to clean a faculty office that happened to be occupied by Dr. Puncky P. Heppner, a professor in Counseling Psychology who was visiting my undergraduate program at the National Taiwan Normal University (NTNU) from the University of Missouri (Mizzou). Dr. Heppner took an interest in me after I chatted with him and explained that I was there to clean his office. Coincidentally, the two programs had just signed a contract and created a new "3+2 Dual Degree Program" (three years of undergraduate studies at NTNU and two years in the master's program at Mizzou). I was actually not that interested in the program when I first heard about it because I was exhausted from all the schooling I'd been through and was questioning whether I actually wanted to be a counselor. I longed to start working so I could be financially independent. But talking to Dr. Heppner and his offers to coach me through the application process, empowered me and I decided to give it a try. I started going to the English Chat Room at NTNU to sharpen my speaking skills. I also worked with my classmate and friend, Diego, to practice our TOEFL test-taking skills, essay writing, and mock interviews. Both my circumstances and the people I connected with were essential in helping me make an important choice in my career, which changed the trajectory of the rest of my life.

The next question people tend to ask is how I ended up in a doctoral program. I really thought I'd go back to Taiwan after my master's program. During my time at Mizzou, I realized the reason I questioned if I could be a counselor was because talking about feelings in Mandarin did not feel natural to me, and that I process my emotions in English (which shouldn't have been a surprise since I've been keeping a diary in English since I was nine). At Mizzou, I was more excited about what I was learning, and I became very familiar with the resources that the school and surrounding community had to offer. Importantly, I felt connected, seen, and understood by my advisor, Dr. Kenneth T. Wang who, growing up between cultures, had a similar background to mine. Dr. Wang helped me realize that research could be fun and relevant to my experience as an international student. Working with him and his other students, a new researcher/scholar identity started to emerge within me. These experiences helped me see I might have what it took to be in a doctoral program, so I applied.

Being in a doctoral program came with a different set of expectations than my master's program. In the doctoral program at Indiana University, I was expected to be able to manage my time between going to classes as a full-time student, working part-time as a graduate assistant, providing therapy to clients, and doing research. It was hard to find a balance and make sure that I was still taking care of myself, especially during my second year when I was commuting 1.5 hours one-way from Bloomington to Indianapolis twice a week to see clients at Indiana University-Purdue University Indianapolis (IUPUI) . There were times when I questioned if I could finish my studies and worried that I was going to let myself, my family, and my community down. When I think back to my time in doctoral studies, I still wonder how I was able to persist despite all the challenges. One thing I am sure of is that I am grateful for the mentors, peers, and friends who believed in and supported me through these hard times by generously sharing their own journeys and resources.

Throughout my studies, and now as a faculty member, multiple prospective international students have reached out seeking advice and mentorship. I wondered why more information was not readily available. This guide was created to share some of the wisdom that I received from my research participants, mentors, and other international students, as well as resources that I benefited from as an international student.

My hope is that this guide helps you navigate higher education proactively so that you not only survive but, most importantly, THRIVE as an international student in the U.S.

Warmly,

Lei Wang, Ph.D.

P.S. Visit www.iTHRIVEbook.com for downloadable worksheets and links to resources. I will be updating the resources periodically.

Contents

Getting Started

This section of the guide addresses everything prior to your arrival in the U.S., from deciding if studying in the U.S. is right for you, to logistics after you've been accepted.

How to use this section of the book:

- If you are at the beginning stages of considering whether to study abroad, start here: *Chapter 1: Why do I want to study in the U.S.?*

- If you have decided that studying in the U.S. is the best choice for you, start here: *Chapter 2: Now that I've decided that I want to pursue an education in the U.S., what's next?*

- If you want tips on how to begin your applications (or interviews), start here: *Chapter 3: Help! What do I do with the applications and interviews?*

- If you are hearing back from schools/programs, start here: *Chapter 4: Congratulations! You're done with applications!!!*

- If you have selected the school/program you will attend, start here: *Chapter 5: Planning ahead: Connecting with current students, securing housing, purchasing textbooks, and making travel plans*

Chapter 1

Why do I want to study in the U.S.?

This chapter includes:

- Reflection questions to determine if studying abroad, especially in the U.S., is the best choice for you.

To make the most of this chapter, reflect:

- What time can you dedicate to working on this chapter, so you can make an informed decision about your future?

"Why do I want to study in the U.S.?" This is one of the most crucial questions to ask yourself. Studying in the U.S. will require investing a lot of time, money, and energy, so you should have some degree of certainty that it's the path you want to take. This is your path, I encourage you to work through this chapter on your own, before discussing it with others.

Take a moment and reflect on why you want to study in the U.S. and what goals you'd like to accomplish.

Example:

I want to study abroad because the U.S. offers more programs/ schools in my field of interest.

I want to be a global citizen by exposing myself to diversity.

Reason/Goal 1:

_____

_____

Reason/Goal 2:

_____

_____

Reason/Goal 3:

_____

_____

Reason/Goal 4:

_____

_____

Reason/Goal 5:

_____

_____

For reference, here are some of the top reasons international students pursue a degree in the U.S.:

- Reputation of schools/programs in the U.S.[1]

- Flexibility and versatility of majors and degrees

- Campus life and state-of-the-art facilities

- Learning environment that fosters independence

- Cultural diversity[2]

Now that you've seen why other international students pursue a degree in the U.S., would you add anything else to your list?

Pros and Cons Exercise

The next step is to weigh the pros and cons of the options you're considering, whether that's studying in the U.S., studying in your home country, or studying in another country.

Example:

Pros of Studying in the U.S.	Cons of Studying in the U.S.
Schools/programs I am interested in are internationally reputable.	I will be away from my friends and family for at least a few years.
More programs to choose from.	Tuition is expensive; unsure whether I will get funding from the school/program.
Some programs have funding for international students.	U.S. schools/programs are less likely to have extensive networking and job placement support in my home country.

---

1   https://www.mastersportal.com/articles/839/5-reasons-why-everyone-wants-to-study-in-the-us.html
    https://www.mastersportal.com/articles/1216/7-reasons-why-students-think-usa-is-the-holy-grail-of-higher-education.html
    2   Check out Open Doors Data at https://opendoorsdata.org/ to find out where other international students come from and the top U.S. institutions that host international students.

Pros of Studying in the U.S.	Cons of Studying in the U.S.
New experiences in a different culture.	It may take me a while to adapt what I learn in the U.S. to the norms and expectations of the field in my home country.
The schools I am interested in have a large international student population.	English is not my native language and learning to navigate daily life in a different language will take time.

Now it's your turn to list the pros and cons of studying in the U.S.

List as many examples as possible. There are no right or wrong answers; this exercise is based on your own circumstances and values.

Pros of Studying in the U.S.	Cons of Studying in the U.S.

It can also be helpful to talk to someone who has recently studied or is studying in the U.S., to get an idea of what their experience as an international student has been like. Keep in mind that the experiences they share are from their perspective; you won't have the exact same ones.

If you're considering studying elsewhere, list the pros and cons for those countries too.

Pros of Studying in _____ [country A]	Cons of Studying in _____ [country A]

Pros of Studying in _____ [country B]	Cons of Studying in _____ [country B]

This is also a good time to consider how your reasons/goals intersect with your options.

For example, maybe the U.S. offers more programs in your field than your home country does but the tuition might be more expensive in the U.S. However, the pros of studying in the U.S. outweigh the cons because you will be a competitive candidate for jobs in companies/organizations you want to work for.

Now, I encourage you to take a break before you conclude what your best option is.

Once you've taken some time to process, write out your conclusion:

I (want to/do not want to) study in the U.S. because _____

_____

_____

After reading this chapter, reflect:

- How do you feel about the conclusion you came to?
- What questions do you still have?

Chapter 2

Now that I've decided that I want to pursue an education in the U.S., what's next?

This chapter includes:

- Building a support system as you apply to schools in the U.S.

- What to consider when you are researching various schools and programs.

- A sample spreadsheet to give you an idea of how to track the information.

To make the most of this chapter, reflect:

- What are some important considerations when choosing schools/programs?

It can be helpful to consider who you want to include on this journey. Research suggests that telling people about your plans and updating them on your progress can help to facilitate success. This step can provide accountability and alleviate feelings of isolation when dealing with the stress and uncertainty of applications. Take a moment to list a few people who can empower and support you in various ways:

Example:

Mom. My mom was an international student herself so she can support me emotionally and in tangible ways.

1 _____

_____

_____

2 _____

_____

_____

3 _____

_____

_____

Once you've decided that you want to study in the U.S, and you've established a "support team," you'll need to decide between schools/programs. Below, I discuss several indicators that set different schools/programs apart. My advice is to read and reread this section to determine what aspects you'll consider when comparing different schools/programs.

The next step is to do more research on the schools/programs that you may be interested in. This can be a lot of information; use an Excel spreadsheet to keep track of your research. A sample spreadsheet is included at the end of this section. I would also encourage you to schedule time to do this research; it can be quite time-consuming but it's an important step.

Below are some indicators to consider as you do your research:

School and Program Rankings

It is important to consider not only the prestige and reputation of the school but also the department(s) and specific program(s) you're interested in. Sometimes it may be better to choose a school with a lower overall ranking but with a more highly ranked department/program because the department/program may have more resources related to your field of study (e.g., funding, labs, equipment). Some governments may offer funding for citizens who study in other countries; however, they may ask for evidence of the ranking of the school and program. You can check out U.S. News Rankings[3] for more details.

Job Prospects

Due to the nature of visa issues, international students typically have to be a few steps ahead.

You should consider the job prospects of the major(s) you are interested in. This information may be readily available on the program's website or you might need to email the admissions or program director to request information about the careers and positions alumni pursue upon graduation.

I would recommend planning your career backward. If you're interested in a professional field that requires licensure (e.g., mental health counselor, lawyer, psychologist, certified public accountant), it should be a part of your consideration. For example, if you're applying to an undergraduate degree program in the U.S. and you're interested in becoming a Licensed Professional Counselor, you'll want to know what undergraduate majors (e.g., psychology) typically help you get into a counseling master's program. Then you'll want to learn about the programs that will allow you to become a Licensed Professional Counselor. In the U.S., licenses are typically state-specific and may require additional supervised hours post-master's degree. This is an important consideration for international students in programs that are coded as non-STEM programs. Such students can apply for a one-year "optional practical training" (OPT) extension to their student visa before they graduate. After that time, they'll have to find an employer to hire them on a work visa (e.g., H1B) to continue to work in the U.S. to accrue hours. International students in programs that are coded as a STEM program can extend their OPT up to 3 years from graduation, which can relieve some of the pressure of finding an employer who will sponsor a work visa. To find out whether a program is coded

---

3   https://www.usnews.com/best-colleges

as STEM, you can email the Office of International Services. There is a lot to consider and planning backward with your goal in mind can help you ask the right questions.

Since most international students go back to their home countries after graduation, it may be important to consider if the U.S. school/program is recognized in your home country. One way to research this is to identify organizations or companies where you might like to work in the future and look into the schools/programs that their employees graduated from. The schools might be listed in staff bios or LinkedIn profiles[4]. This process will help you identify what schools/programs are known in your home country and give you a sense of what educational level (bachelor's, master's, doctorate, certificate, etc.) will help you to be a competitive candidate.

List the pros and cons of going back home, staying in the U.S., or going to another country to seek career opportunities upon graduation:

Pros of Working in _____ [country A]	Cons of Working in _____ [country A]

---

4   https://www.linkedin.com

Pros of Working in _____ [country B]	Cons of Working in the _____ [country B]

Pros of Working in _____ [country C]	Cons of Working in _____ [country C]

Costs and Funding Opportunities

Let's be honest: studying in the U.S. can be quite expensive! Without external funding, international students typically pay out-of-state tuition and additional international fees. Unfortunately, most U.S. financial aid and work-study programs are not available to international students. You might want to see if there are scholarships available at the schools you are considering. You can usually find information about scholarships on departmental, Dean of Students, and Office of International Services' websites. Make sure the scholarships are available to international students and/or students from your country-of-origin. If the information is not readily available, don't give up! Email faculty and staff to inquire.

Graduate students should also explore opportunities to be a graduate assistant (GA), teaching assistant (TA), or research assistant (RA). Job descriptions for these roles vary based on the supervisor and project. Assistantships, depending on the type and funding, may offer tuition remission (100% of tuition is funded) or reduced tuition (partial tuition is funded). Home-country governmental scholarships may also be available but may be limited to certain fields of study.

Beyond these opportunities, international students are generally restricted to part-time on-campus work. Often this means up to 20 hours/week during the fall and spring semesters and up to 40 hours/week during the summer. It can be helpful to look at work-study opportunities outside of your program. These might be available in other departments or offices (e.g., Dean of Students, Multicultural Center, Residential Life). You may want to check the school's Human Resources webpage and Career Center(s) to find listings. Typically, these job openings are posted at the end of the fall semester for the following fall semester and the relevant office will interview candidates until mid-spring semester. Sometimes job openings pop up suddenly due to grant funding, so be sure to check regularly outside of the typical timeline.

Assistantships and scholarships may be very competitive, and it can be difficult to get one in your first year. If you are unable to secure such funding, you can always wait until you are in the U.S. and then apply for a part-time position in the dining halls, residence halls, library, or school bookstore, where you can make an hourly wage. Once you have a stronger network on campus, it might be worth reapplying for scholarships and assistantships.

Another option is to research nearby community colleges that offer similar coursework. It is common for domestic students to take classes at a community college and then transfer those credits to a bigger university. This way, students can save on tuition (community colleges tend to be more affordable) and still earn a degree from a larger institution.

International Student Population on Campus

Another consideration is the international student population. Schools with more international students may have more tailored resources (e.g., mental health counselors who speak various languages, immigration lawyers to consult with close to graduation), professors may have more experience with and a better understanding of the unique needs of international students (e.g., visa restrictions), and there may be more international restaurants and supermarkets nearby. Open Doors Data from the Institute of International Education[5] can provide more detail on the number of international students by country of origin, school, etc. It may also be helpful to use Google Maps to check out the surrounding neighborhoods, stores, and shops to get a sense of what the environment is like.

Current Students' Experiences

It is important to talk to current students about their experiences. Reach out to the Office of International Services and ask to speak to another international student. If there are no international students in the program you are interested in, ask to speak to an American student in the program as well as an international student in the same department. The school/program may also refer you to an alumnus; if possible, try to speak to someone who graduated recently to get a current view of the experience. Some questions that you can consider asking are:

- What has been your overall experience studying at the school/program? Would you recommend the school/program to others? Why or why not?

- How would you describe the culture at the school/program? Do people get along? Do most professors have an open-door policy (allow you to drop by their office) or require you to schedule an appointment?

- How do you like the community surrounding the school? Do you feel safe/welcomed? Are you able to find food/ingredients from your culture at restaurants or supermarkets?

- Can you tell me about your experience living on/off campus? How is the public transportation there?

- What do you wish you would've known prior to studying at the school/program?

---

[5] https://opendoorsdata.org/

Professors and Research Interests

You might want to look up the professors in the programs you're considering and read about their research. This is especially important for students applying to graduate programs at research-intensive universities. Sometimes programs accept students based on whether certain professors are taking advisees. If there are specific professors you are interested in working with, it may be helpful to find out if they are taking students in the upcoming academic year. You can write them an email explaining who you are, what your research interests are, and asking if they are taking students. Here is an example of an email request:

Subject: Interest in Applying to _____ Program

Dear Dr. _____,
I hope this email finds you well. I am writing to introduce myself and express interest in applying to the _____ program. My name is _____ and my research interests are_____. [Briefly talk about how your research and the professor's interests overlap.]
I am interested in working with you and was wondering if you are taking doctoral students in the upcoming academic year.
I look forward to hearing back from you. Thank you!
Best,
[your name]

In some fields, it is common to request to schedule time to speak with the professor over Skype/Zoom because they may prefer to answer questions verbally rather than spending a lot of time responding to emails. During such a meeting, you can ask about funding opportunities for international students and if any assistantship positions were held by international students historically. These meetings may seem daunting, but they can be extremely informative and give you a glimpse of the personality of the professor and how they work with international students. Remember, it's just a glimpse and first impressions are not always accurate. Ensure you're prepared for these meetings by listing any questions that you have. It might also be helpful to practice with a friend first if you are worried about your mannerisms and performance (e.g., making "eye contact" by looking into the camera).

After reading this chapter, reflect:

- What are some aspects of U.S. schools/programs you have not considered and would like to include in your search?

- How would you rank the importance of these various aspects (e.g., prestige of school, international student population) to help you narrow down the schools/programs you apply to?

As you do this research, record the information in an Excel spreadsheet. This will allow you to easily compare the schools/programs you're considering. Here is an example of what the spreadsheet might look like:

	School/ Program 1	School/ Program 2	School/ Program 3
Application Deadline/Fees			
Application Portal Website/ Account/Password			
SAT/ACT/GRE Requirement/Score			
TOEFL Requirement/Score			
Application Materials			
US News Ranking			
International Student Population			
Office of International Affairs Contact Information			
Program Contact Information			
Potential Advisor's Name & Contact Information (for graduate school)			
Potential Advisor's Research (for graduate school)			
Funding Available for International Students			
Tuition Costs Per Credit/Total Costs			
Cost of Living in the City[6]			
Current Student Contact Information			
Average Years to Receive Degree			
Home Country Governmental Scholarships Available			
Letter of Recommendation Requirement			

---

6   To estimate the cost of living, you can Google "cost of living calculator." Some calculators will also allow you to compare cities.

Chapter 3

Help! What do I do with the applications and interviews?

This chapter includes:

- Tips on how to prepare for standardized tests and English proficiency tests.

- Putting together a resume and/or curriculum vitae (CV).

- Writing application essays.

- Requesting letters of recommendation.

- Preparing for interviews and tips on the most common interview questions.

- Sample CV.

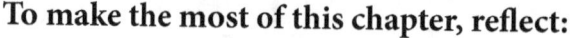

To make the most of this chapter, reflect:

- While you were researching programs, what application requirements surprised you?

Use the spreadsheet you created in the last section to guide you when narrowing down the schools/programs to apply to. There is no magic number for how many places to apply; it's really about applying to places that are a good fit for you (e.g., being in the program can help you achieve your career goals) and where you are a good fit for the program (e.g., you are what they are looking for and can add value to the program). For example, I applied to seven Ph.D. programs, received two interviews, and was accepted into one program. Some people apply to 12-15 places to increase the chance of being offered interviews and acceptance. It also depends on your budget and how much you're willing to spend on the application process — it can add up!

Now that you've finalized a list of potential schools/programs, let's talk about how to prepare for your applications.

Standardized Tests and English Proficiency Tests

Most schools will ask you to submit your English proficiency test results and (a) Scholastic Aptitude Test (SAT) or American College Test (ACT) scores if you are applying to undergraduate programs; or (b) Graduate Record Examinations (GRE), GRE Subject Test, Graduate Management Admission Test (GMAT), Law School Admission Test (LSAT), or Medical College Admission Test (MCAT) depending on what graduate program you are applying to. Every program will have different requirements for the scores. While English as a Foreign Language (TOEFL iBT) is the most popular English proficiency test, some schools and programs may accept your test scores from International English Language Testing System (IELTS), Test of English for International Communication (TOEIC), or Duolingo's English Test so be sure to double-check before you register for the test. The trick to standardized testing is mastering test-taking techniques. There are plenty of standardized test and English proficiency test preparation books available; I encourage you to stick to one book for each test. Trying to study using multiple sources may lead to more confusion. I used the Princeton Review to study for the GRE. Whichever books you choose, the most important thing is to have a study schedule. Make sure you complete the practice tests and fully understand each question, especially the ones where you guessed or made a mistake.

Many international students worry about their English-speaking skills on the English proficiency test. Don't let anxiety become a barrier to your performance! My suggestion is to practice, practice, and practice! If you are in high school or pursuing an undergraduate degree, befriend your English instructor and practice speaking to them in English. If you have a classmate who speaks English well, don't be shy, ask them to practice with you. If you are not currently in school, you may want to take English conversation classes in person or online so you can get more comfortable using the language. For the English proficiency test, if you are admitted to the school with a score lower than the threshold, the school will likely ask you to take some English classes before taking classes in your major. You might be able to waive the English proficiency test if you have already studied in the U.S. for another degree.

Because of the COVID-19 pandemic, some schools and programs waived their standardized test requirements. This saves time and money for applicants and forces admissions teams to consider each student based on their essays and what they bring to the program. Remember to check to see if the requirement is waived for the schools/programs you are applying for.

Resume and Curriculum Vitae (CV)

The main difference between a resume and a CV is that a resume is typically one to two pages long whereas a CV has no page limit and should include everything you have done in the academic field. Typically, schools will ask for your CV. Two key things to keep in mind for resumes and CVs are consistency in formatting (e.g., using the same font, bolding or italicizing job titles, etc.) and using strong action verbs to highlight what you did. If you submit a resume or CV to apply for assistantships or scholarships, try your best to match the formatting of a standard American resume or CV. See the end of this section for a sample CV. More tips and examples of resumes and CVs are available on career center webistes, such as the University of Missouri's Career Center webpage.[7]

Application Essays

Refer to the spreadsheet you created and review why you are excited about the schools/programs you are applying to. Give specific examples about how your experiences/interests align with the schools' offerings. Programs are looking for students who are a good fit with them (e.g., career path, research interests with professors). You do not need to have the exact same research interest as a professor, however, having some relation to their areas of expertise can help them guide you in your research. For example, one of my research areas is mental health among Asian international students. A student collaborating with me had an interest in student-athletes, so we combined our interests to study the experiences of international student-athletes.

---

[7]   https://career.missouri.edu/resumes-cover-letters/writing-a-resume/

I want to emphasize the importance of having someone look over your essays before you submit them. You want to strive for no spelling or grammatical errors in your essays! One option could be utilizing editing services in your home country to correct grammatical/spelling errors. Tools like Grammarly or ChatGPT can also help to correct such as errors. You could also ask current students in the program to provide you with some feedback. If you feel shy or don't want to burden current students, I'd encourage you to step outside your comfort zone; the worst thing they can do is say no to your request.

Letters of Recommendation

Asking for letters of recommendation will take some planning on your part. First, you need to identify three to five people who can speak to your work. It would be best to **not** have letters from parents, friends, clergy members, or therapists. It's always good to have a backup or two in case someone is unable or unwilling to write a letter for you. Consider asking professors from classes you did well in or employers who can speak to your skills and work ethic. Always ask if they can write you a strong, positive letter, give them plenty of time to do it (at least a few weeks), and remind them when deadlines are coming up. Take a proactive approach to help recommenders write strong and positive letters: send a draft of your application essays, a list of schools/programs/professors you are applying to (an Excel spreadsheet may be helpful), and a bullet point list of things you'd like them to highlight (e.g., strengths, experiences). Sometimes letter writers might ask you to write your own recommendation letters, which may feel somewhat awkward. If that happens, start by Googling sample letters. Pretending you're writing the letter for a friend might help you highlight positive aspects of yourself and avoid being overly humble.

Interview

Some programs include interviews in the application process. Be aware of any relevant time difference to ensure the proposed times work for you. If the proposed time is an odd hour for you, tell the person who contacted you so they can help you to reschedule; programs should not expect you to wake up at 3 am to participate.

Here are some common graduate school interview questions and my suggestions on how to craft your answer:

1. *Tell me about yourself.*

Students I have worked with consistently report this as one of the hardest questions to respond to. How do you stand out from the rest of the interviewees in the brief amount of time given? I suggest using the first sentence to state your name and educational background.

Follow up with your interest in the program and then make the explanation more personal (something the interviewer may not be able to assume just from your CV or resume). Finally, end with something you'd like the interviewer to remember you by or ask more about.

For example, when I was interviewing for Ph.D. programs, I would say something like, "My name is Lei Wang and I am a master's student in Counseling Psychology at the University of Missouri. I am originally from Taiwan and in my time in the U.S., I've learned that I'm very interested in doing research, especially on the experiences of international students and their adjustment to American culture. Clinically, I have a strong interest in working with students from historically marginalized communities. I would like to gain more experience at the department training clinic and be involved in the wider campus community."

2. *What are your career goals?*

Even if you are not sure what you would like to do, sharing your current goals helps the interviewer assess whether the program can help you get where you want to be (this is where the fit between you and the program comes in). When I was applying to doctoral programs, I was about 70% sure that I wanted to see clients as a counseling psychologist at a university counseling center. However, in my fourth year as a doctoral student, as I enjoyed the balance of teaching, research, and counseling clients, my career goals began to shift. In my fifth year, my full-time internship at a counseling center solidified my desire to work as a faculty member. You're allowed to change your mind but having a plan can help you appear more focused in the interview.

3. *Where do you see yourself in 5/10/15 years?*

This question is meant to assess your career goals. Again, these plans do not have to be set in stone. As an international student, it can be difficult to plan a career trajectory because there is no certainty about where you may end up, especially with changing immigration laws. To respond to this question, consider how to combine your ideal scenario and what is realistic into an answer that feels genuine.

4. *What are your research/clinical interests?*

These questions should be relatively straightforward. This is a good time to mention the professors you think you would work well with. It may be helpful to look up the professor's recent publications (the last 3 years) to get an idea of what they have been up to and so you can easily recall some information about their recent work.

5. *Field-specific questions.*

Programs will want to evaluate your competence in areas that are pertinent to your field. For instance, in counseling psychology, applicants are often presented with a clinical case and asked how they might conceptualize and work with the client. For STEM-related fields, you may be asked for solutions to certain problems. Typically, programs will let you know what to expect before the interview. However, it doesn't hurt to search the internet for the types of questions you may encounter. Even better, ask current students for tips on preparing for the interview.

6. **Random personal questions.**

For example, "What is the last non-academic book you read?" "If you had to use an animal to describe yourself, what would it be?" Sometimes interviewers may include one or two questions that appear to be out of place as a way to learn more about you. This is also a way for them to see how you react when you are asked to think on your feet. It is always okay to tell your interviewer, "That's a great question; let me think about it," before you answer.

7. **Do you have any questions for us?**

This important question is typically saved until the end of the interview. Make sure you come to the interview with a few questions to show your interest and that you have done research on the program. Questions I have asked include, "How would you describe the culture between faculty and students in the program?" "What are some things that you enjoy about living in this city?" "How would you describe your mentoring style?" and "What qualities do you typically look for in a student?" Be mindful that this is not the time to ask the interviewers how you performed in the interview.

When giving examples to support your answers, you may want to consider the STAR method. STAR stands for situation, task, action, and result. For example, if the question is *"Please describe a weakness you have."* I might answer like this:

- Situation: "It takes me a while to process my reactions, especially when faced with difficult situations or when I am in a group setting."

- Task: "This posed a challenge in class discussions because by the time I found the words to describe my thoughts, the class had already moved onto another topic."

- Action: "In order to increase my participation, I decided to write down my reactions to the readings, even if it was just one bullet point."

- Result: "This helped me to feel more prepared because I didn't have to worry about coming up with an answer in the moment. I was more inclined to speak up in class because I was less afraid of being judged when I did so."

Practice, practice, practice! This is the same advice I gave to American students when I worked at a career center. Make sure you look up other commonly asked interview questions for your field and come up with a few things to say. It may be helpful to write your responses in bullet points, instead of full paragraphs, so you don't end up reading them. Keep your responses concise (30-60 seconds) and direct (e.g., following the STAR method), so that interviewers can easily follow along.

Finally, the interview is not over until you send a short and engaging thank-you email. Be sure to note the interviewers' names. Their email addresses should be available on the program's website. If that information is not readily available, you can contact the administrative assistant and politely request that your email be forwarded. Beyond expressing gratitude for the interviewers' time, this is a good opportunity to mention something that stood out to you during the interview, which can help the interviewers remember who you are. Here is an example of a thank-you email that you would send a day or two after the interview:

> Subject: Thank You for Your Time!
> Dear Dr. _____,
> Thank you for taking the time to interview me on [date]. I am very excited about this potential opportunity to work with you and other faculty members for the next few years. Specifically, I look forward to working on _____. I believe that with your mentorship, I will be able to contribute to the field in significant ways while moving toward my career goals. Thank you again and I hope to hear back from the program soon!
> Sincerely,
> [Your Name]

After reading this chapter, reflect:

- What aspects of the application process make you feel stressed, nervous, or anxious?

- What will you need to put your applications together successfully? What are you already prepared for?

- Who can review your applications before you submit them?

- What resources can you identify to help you practice interviews? (If relevant)

Here is an example of what my CV looked like when I first applied for Ph.D. programs. Afterwards, I provide an updated version of the same CV where I explain what changes I made and why.

Lei Wang
phone number • email address • mailing address
Google Scholar: https://tinyurl.com/LWscholar • LinkedIn: https://www.linkedin.com/in/drleiwang

Education

University of Missouri   Columbia, Missouri
Master of Education in Counseling Psychology   GPA: 3.94/4.00, Aug 2011-May 2014
       3+2 Dual Degree Program
National Taiwan Normal University   Taipei, Taiwan
Bachelor of Arts in Educational Psychology & Counseling   GPA: 88.52/100.00, Sept 2009-June 2011

Clinical and Volunteer Experiences

Multicultural Career Consultant, University of Missouri International Student Career Services
Columbia, Missouri   September 2012-May 2013

- Served a total of 152 hours, 3 events, attended 14 hours of group supervision, 14 hours of staff meetings and received a semester-long weekly 2-hour training with undergraduate Career Specialists on Career Center resources and practical helping skills.
- Co-conducted 4 workshops including "Campus Survival English," "Resume, CV and Cover Letter," and "Basic/Advanced Interviewing Skills."
- Utilized multicultural/cross-cultural sensitivity to facilitate career-related conversations with international/domestic students and referred them to relevant resources.
- Applied career assessments, reviewed resumes, curriculum vitae, and cover letters during individual consultation hours.

Peer Educator/Staffer, University of Missouri Relationship and Sexual Violence Prevention Center
Columbia, Missouri   August 2012-February 2013

- Served a total of 65 hours and 7 events (including tabling, Rock Against Rape, Clothesline project, STARS Speak, etc.), attended 22 hours of weekly staff meetings, and completed 2 promotional videos.
- Completed "Ask. Listen. Refer." online suicide prevention training on September 7, 2012.
- Certified in Bystander Prevention by the Green Dot Conference on September 29, 2012 and February 9, 2013.
- Established familiarity with the importance of support and sensitivity to empower violence survivors through coursework, ex. ESC_PS 7087 "Relationship and Sexual Violence Prevention"

(peer educator program) and Dr. Bryana French's ESC_PS 7087 "Violence Against Women and Children".

Volunteer Counselor, Rotary International MG Project

Taipei, Taiwan   September 2008-June 2010

- Attended 10 training sessions (total of 20 hours) on practical counseling skills for work with K-12 foster children.
- Counseled 3 Taiwanese adolescents (7th, 8th and 9th graders; 2 males and 1 female) for 3 semesters, 10 times/semester (once per week).
- Trained to conduct case/progress notes and immediate transcriptions of counseling session.
- Received a total of 8 group supervision sessions over 3 semesters, led by 3 advanced graduate students from the Department of Education Psychology and Counseling.

Teaching and Outreach Experiences

Graduate Assistant, University of Missouri International Students' Career Services

Columbia, Missouri   August 2013-May 2014

- Dedicated a total of 303 hours, attended 10 hours of individual supervision, 4 hours of group supervision, 15 hours of staff meetings and 11 hours of large group meetings with undergraduate Career Specialists.
- Planned, marketed, screened participants and co-facilitated an interactive eight-week International Students' Job Search Connection Group. Tailored offerings to meet group needs regarding U.S.-based job search. Incorporated activities to allow the 5 members to educate and offer emotional support to each other.
- Fostered collaboration among different departments and organizations, such as the Graduate School, International Teaching Assistant Program, Chinese Business Students Association, Society of Manufacturing Engineers, AIESEC, and Engineering Career Services via programming.
- Planned, marketed, and screened participants for an eight-week International Students' Cultural Transition group.
- Coordinated and conducted 8 career-related workshops for international students, including "On-Campus Part-Job Search", "Resume, CV and Cover Letter Writing Skills", "Interviewing Skills", "Graduate School Application", and "Applying for Full-Time Jobs and Immigration Status".
- Provided individual consultation to international and domestic students regarding career exploration and decisions.
- Mentored 2 new graduate assistants and familiarized them with the work environment and materials.
- Co-led a monthly Cross-Cultural Connection Group on cultural barriers and coping strategies with the Women's Center graduate assistant and staff.
- Represented International Students' Career Services through 2 outreach-tabling events (Interna-

tional Student Orientation and International Welcome Party), 2 meetings (Missouri International Student Council and Graduate School Professional Development), and 3 presentations (International Student Orientation, Asian American Association and Multicultural Hour).

Dual Degree Program Graduate Assistant, Dr. Puncky Heppner

Columbia, Missouri

March 2012-May 2013

- Collaborated with faculty members, Drs. Puncky Heppner, Kenneth Wang, and Barbara Williamson to prepare prospective Taiwanese students on topics including housing, course registration, and English improvement.
- Designed and facilitated Dual Degree Program orientation workshop session "Friends: American, Taiwanese and Other Internationals" to prepare Taiwanese students on cross-cultural awareness and knowledge of relevant resources on-campus.
- Served as a mentor for 7 incoming Counseling Psychology students from Taiwan and provided guidance and support on academic achievement and extracurricular experiences.

English Tutor, Freelance

Taipei, Taiwan

March 2009-August 2012

- Taught 5 students aged12-35, including English class previews and reviews, TOEFL, IELTS, and preparation for graduate school applications.
- Established a safe and trusting environment for students to explore English without fear of being judged or evaluated.
- Organized and tailored lesson plans according to students' English competency levels and needs.

Leadership and Service Experiences

Vice President of Communications, AIESEC-Mizzou

Columbia, Missouri

January 2013-December 2013

- Implemented a new project management platform for the communications department.
- Managed a team of 12 to streamline internal communications and external branding of a non-profit student-run business, including:

  -Establishing relationship with marketing channels in Columbia, St. Louis, and Kansas City.

  -Organizing events with local businesses and outreach to the student and community population.

  -Delivering newsletters to students (bi-monthly), AIESEC alumni (quarterly) and members (weekly).

  -Maintaining social media platforms including website, LinkedIn, Podio, Twitter and Facebook.

  -Tracking customers satisfaction with AIESEC international internship service.

  -Holding weekly meetings with staff members and conducting member education seminars, retreats, and socials.

- Released team leader and member applications to organization members, screened candidates for motivation, potential, qualifications, and fit for the positions and team culture.

- Represented the organization through consistent branding by responding to emails from students, faculty, and parents in a prompt manner.
- Maintained transparency of executive decisions by taking executive board and communications team meeting minutes and posting them on Podio.
- Increased synergy by collaborating with other departments, including Talent Management on recruitment for local committee members (via Summer Welcome tabling, newsletters, handouts, etc.), Outgoing Exchange on recruitment for students to volunteer abroad, Incoming Exchange on planning and hosting the "Columbia on the Map: Business Leadership and Development Luncheon," developing professional materials and LinkedIn training.

Curriculum Chair, Rotary International MG Project
Taipei, Taiwan   June 2010-July 2011
- Attended a total of 12 monthly meetings with 6 fellow coordinators and 2 graduate-level supervisors to revise and improve progress in order to cater to the needs of the organization.
- Prepared undergraduate volunteer counselors through trainings with guest speakers, including an introduction to 4 partner children's shelters, basic counseling skills, and themed workshops (ex. separation, relationships, counselor's mindfulness, and picture book therapy).
- Developed surveys for volunteers to provide feedback and analyzed results for improvement.
- Presented annual results at an end-of-term business luncheon for corporate sponsors in order to continue partnership and funding.

Research Experiences
Team Member, Dr. Kenneth Wang's Research Team
Columbia, Missouri   August 2011-May 2014
- Mentored 1 doctoral and 2 first-year master's students on research processes, such as brainstorming for research questions, utilization of conceptual framework, related scales selection, IRB training, Qualtrics survey system, participant recruitment strategies, data cleaning procedures, and APA proposal submission on comparing the experiences of Asian Americans and Asian international college students.
- Co-translated a total of 4 scales from English into Mandarin Chinese, including Self-Reflection and Insight Scale (SRIS; Grant, Franklin, & Langford, 2002), Multigroup Ethnic Identity Measure (MEIM-II; Roberts, Phinney, Masse, Chen, Roberts, & Romero, 1999), Grit Scale (Duckworth, Peterson, Matthews, & Kelly, 2007) and Subjective Happiness Scale (SHS; Lyubomirsky & Lepper, 1999).
- Back-translated a total of 4 scales from Mandarin Chinese into English, including Career Factors Inventory (CFI; Rottinghaus, Day, & Borgen, 2005), Vocational Outcome Expectation Scale-Revised (VOE-R; Metheny & McWhirter, 2013), Career Search Efficacy Scale (CSES; Solberg et al., 1994), Sense of Control Scale (SOC; Lachman & Weaver, 1998), and Acculturation Index (AI;

Ward & Kennedy, 1994).

- Organized research literature database on international students' cross-cultural well-being, coping skills, and adjustment processes using Endnote and Excel.
- Peer-reviewed team members' research proposals and manuscript drafts.
- Received training on IBM SPSS (ANOVA, regression, factor analysis), M+ (Latent Profile Analysis, Growth Mixture Modeling), IRB, literature search and review, APA style academic writing (how to write intro, literature review, methods, results), poster presentation, and conference etiquette.
- Participated in the process of developing a scale to measure international students' cross-cultural losses and designing a website for professional international students, including literature review and other subjects of matter.

Research Assistant, Dr. Yi-Fen Su's Research Team

Taipei, Taiwan

April 2009-August 2011

- Transcribed 50 hours+ qualitative data in Mandarin Chinese.
- Assisted with keying-in grade one-through-twelve children's survey data on developing Chinese reading ability tests.
- Established familiarity with the study of children with reading disabilities.

Professional Publications
Peer-Reviewed Journal Articles

- Wang, L., Wang, K. T., Heppner, P. P., & Chuang, C.-C. (under review). Cross-national cultural competency among Taiwanese international students. Journal of Diversity in Higher Education. Advance online publication. doi:10.1037/dhe0000020
- Wang, K. T., Heppner, P. P., Wang, L., & Zhu, F. (2014). Cultural intelligence trajectories in new international students: Implications for the development of cross-cultural competence. International Perspectives in Psychology: Research, Practice, Consultation, 4, 51-65. doi:10.1037/ipp0000027

Peer-Reviewed Conference Presentations & Symposia

- Wang, L., Wang, K. T., & Chuang, C.-C. (2013, August). Predictors and outcomes of cross-national cultural competency among international students. Paper presented at the American Psychological Association Annual Convention, Honolulu, Hawaii.
- Wang, K. T., Heppner, P. P., Wang, L., & Zhu, F. (2013, July). Cultural intelligence, language discrimination and well-being: A 4-Wave longitudinal study. In M. Wei & K. T. Wang (Co-Chairs), Addressing Chinese international students' need: Racial and language discrimination. Symposium presented at the American Psychological Association Annual Convention, Honolulu, Hawaii.

Other Publications

- Wang, L. (2014, February 26). The perks of being an international student [Web log post]. Retrieved from Career Scoop (MU Career Center's blog).

Professional Memberships

American Psychological Association of Graduate Students (APAGS)

Student Affiliate	December 2012-present
APA Ambassador	July 2013-August 2013

Division 17: Society of Counseling Psychology

Student Affiliate	December 2012-present

Division 29: Division of Psychotherapy

Student Affiliate	December 2013-2014

Division 35: Society for the Psychology of Women—Section 5: Psychology for Asian Pacific American Women

Student Affiliate	August 2013-present

Division 52: International Psychology

Campus Student Representative	December 2012-2013

Professional Trainings Received

Safe Space Training, MU LGBTQ Resource Center, 1 session	October 2012
A Taste of Mindfulness, Student Health Center, 6 sessions	February-March 2012
Biofeedback, Student Health Center, 3 sessions	February 2012
Safe Space Training, MU LGBTQ Resource Center, 1 session	November 2011

Scholarships & Honors

University of Missouri

Travel Grant Award, Graduate Student Association	Fall 2013
US Bank Scholarship, Missouri Student Unions	Fall 2013
Nominee, Honor's Society	Summer 2013, Spring 2014, Fall 2014
Student Travel Awards, Department of Educational, School and Counseling Psychology	Summer 2013
Travel Awards, Graduate Professional Council	Summer 2013

National Taiwan Normal University

Dual Degree Scholarship, Ministry of Education	Fall 2011, Spring 2012

Here is an edited version of my CV based on the norms and best practices I know now:

Lei Wang, M.Ed.

Mailing Address

Phone: (xxx) xxx-xxxx
Email: xxxx@xxx.xxx
Google Scholar: https://tinyurl.com/LWscholar

Make sure to have your name in large font at the very top of the page.

EDUCATION

M.Ed.
Expected: May 2014

University of Missouri, Columbia, Missouri
Counseling Psychology, 3+2 Dual Degree Program
Thesis: *Cross-national cultural competency among Taiwanese international students* (Advisor: Kenneth T. Wang, Ph.D.)

B.Ed.
Expected: May 2014

National Taiwan Normal University, Taipei, Taiwan
Educational Psychology and Counseling

My CV is now structured in transparent tables because it is easier to format this way.

RESEARCH INTEREST

My primary research interest is Asian International and Asian American college students' mental health. Specifically, I focus on cultural adjustment, perceived discrimination, career, and mental health outcomes.

You might consider reordering the different sections, so the information that is most relevant for the school/program/job is at the top.

PEER-REVIEWED PUBLICATIONS (1)

Wang, K. T., Heppner, P. P., Wang, L., & Zhu, F. (2014). Cultural intelligence trajectories in new international students: Implications for the development of cross-cultural competence. *International Perspectives in Psychology: Research, Practice, Consultation*, 4(1), 51-65. https://doi.org/10.1037/ipp0000027

MANUSCRIPTS UNDER REVIEW (1)

Wang, L., Wang, K. T., Heppner, P. P., & Chuang, C.-C. (under review). Cross-national cultural competency among Taiwanese international students. *Journal of Diversity in Higher Education*, 10(3), 271-287. https://doi.org/10.1037/dhe0000020

PEER-REVIEWED CONFERENCE PRESENTATIONS (2)

Wang, L., Wang, K. T., & Chuang, C.-C. (2013, August). *Predictors and outcomes of cross-national cultural competency among international students*. Poster presented at the American Psychological Association Annual Convention, Honolulu, Hawaii.

Wang, K. T., Heppner, P. P., Wang, L., & Zhu, F. (2013, July). *Cultural intelligence, language discrimination and well-being: A 4-wave longitudinal study*. In M. Wei & K. T. Wang (Co-Chairs), Addressing Chinese international students' need: Racial and language discrimination. Symposium presented at the American Psychological Association Annual Convention, Honolulu, Hawaii

Group related positions together (both paid and non-paid) and use the headers to reflect what the positions entail.

CLINICAL & COMMUNICATION EXPERIENCES

2013-2014   Graduate Assistant, University of Missouri International Students' Career Services, Columbia, MO
- Planned, marketed, screened and co-facilitated an interactive eight-week International Students' Job Search Connection Group. Tailored offerings to meet group needs regarding U.S.-based job search. Incorporated activities to allow the 5 members to educate and offer emotional support to each other.
- Fostered collaboration among different departments and organizations, such as the Graduate School, International Teaching Assistant Program, Chinese Business Students Association, Society of Manufacturing Engineers, AIESEC, and Engineering Career Services.
- Coordinated and conducted career-related workshops for international students, including "On-Campus Part-Job Search," "Resume, CV and Cover Letter Writing Skill," "Interviewing Skills," "Graduate School Application," and "Applying for Full-Time Jobs and Immigration Status."
- Co-led a monthly Cross-Cultural Connection Group on cultural barriers and coping strategies with the Women's Center graduate assistant and staff.

2012-2013   Multicultural Career Consultant, University of Missouri International Student Career Services, Columbia, MO
- Conducted career assessments, reviewed resumes, curriculum vitae, and cover letters for undergraduate and graduate students.
- Facilitated workshops on "Campus Survival English," "Resume, CV and Cover Letter," and "Basic/Advanced Interviewing Skills."

2012-2013   Dual Degree Program Graduate Assistant, Dr. Puncky Heppner, Columbia, MO
- Designed and facilitated Dual Degree Program orientation workshop session "Friends: American, Taiwanese and Other Internationals" to prepare Taiwanese students on cross-cultural awareness and knowledge of relevant resources on-campus.
- Served as a mentor for 7 incoming Counseling Psychology students from Taiwan and provided guidance and support on academic achievement and extracurricular experiences.

AWARDS, GRANTS, & SCHOLARSHIPS (5)

2013   Travel Grant Award ($200)
Graduate Student Association, University of Missouri

2013   US Bank Scholarship ($500)
Missouri Student Unions, University of Missouri

2013   Student Travel Awards ($400)
Department of Educational, School and Counseling Psychology, University of Missouri

2013   Travel Awards ($300)
Graduate Professional Council, University of Missouri

Depending on your comfort level, you can decide whether to include the $ amount of funding received.

2011-2012	Dual Degree Scholarship ($12,000) Ministry of Education, Taiwan

PROFESSIONAL LEADERSHIP & SERVICE

2013	APA Ambassador, American Psychological Association of Graduate Students
2012-2013	Campus Student Representative, Division 52: International Psychology, American Psychological Association

PROFESSIONAL MEMBERSHIP

2013-2019	Student Affiliate, Division 17: Society of Counseling Psychology, American Psychological Association
2013-2019	Student Affiliate, Section 5: Psychology for Asian Pacific American Women, Division 35: Society for the Psychology of Women, American Psychological Association
2012-2019	Member, American Psychological Association of Graduate Students

VOLUNTEER EXPERIENCES

2012-2013	Peer Educator/Staffer, University of Missouri Relationship and Sexual Violence Prevention Center, Columbia, MO • Completed "Ask. Listen. Refer." online suicide prevention training on September 7, 2012. • Certified in Bystander Prevention by the Green Dot Conference on September 29, 2012 and February 9, 2013. • Took ESC_PS 7087 "Relationship and Sexual Violence Prevention" (peer educator program) and Dr. Bryana French's ESC_PS 7087 "Violence Against Women and Children."

Chapter 4

Congratulations!
You're done with applications!!!

This chapter includes:

- Encouragement to celebrate no matter the outcome.
- Checklist for visa applications.

To make the most of this chapter, reflect:

- How do you feel about the application process? What thoughts or feelings are coming up for you?

Honor Your Efforts

Whether you received acceptance letters, rejection letters, or a combination, I would encourage you to take time to honor the effort and energy that you put into the application process.

Note: It is completely normal to receive rejection letters if this is your first time apply-ing (and even if it's not your first time!). While it may be disappointing, you should still honor your efforts. It is important to give yourself the space to experience your feelings, by yourself or with others.

If you did not receive any acceptance letters (this time), take some time to reflect on if you would like to reapply. If you do, what might you do differently, how could you be a more competitive candidate, and which programs might you apply to next time? Consider reaching out to the programs you already applied to and asking for feedback on how you can prepare yourself to be a stronger candidate if you reapply. Keep in mind that not all programs are willing or able to give specific feedback.

Whether you received acceptance letters or not, make sure you celebrate! This was a long journey; you deserve to enjoy the moment and celebrate how awesome you are and the hard work you put in. And when I say celebrate, I mean CELEBRATE! I strongly encourage you NOT to skip over this step.

Ways that I will celebrate completing the application process:

Example:

I will reward myself by going out for a nice dinner at Ding Tai Feng on Friday night with my family.

1 _____

_____

2 _____

_____

3 _____

_____

After taking some time to celebrate, you need to decide whether to accept your offer(s). If you were accepted to a program, it is important to evaluate if you want to accept the offer. If you were accepted by multiple programs, this is a GOOD problem to have! Revisit and expand your list of pros and cons for each school/program you're considering. This is also a good time to reach out to current students to gain more insight into their experiences.

Visa Applications

While in the U.S., maintaining your student visa status is **critical**, so read, re-read, and triple-read the paperwork. If you accept an offer from a school/program, the Office of International Services or the equivalent office will contact you. This office will be a resource for visa issues for the entirety of your time as an international student.

Research and collect the relevant documentation before making an appointment with the U.S. embassy, consulate, or equivalent office in your country. The information will be available on the consulate's website and, if you have further questions, you can reach out to the Office of International Service or call the U.S. consulate. This process may take some planning, especially if the consulate is not located in your city and would require you to travel and perhaps even stay overnight. Check for the earliest available appointment time that works with your schedule and start the process as soon as possible to maximize your chances of receiving the visa on time. Sometimes American consulates give priority to people applying for student visas. Double-check what you can and cannot bring into the consulate, and if there are lockers available on site. I made the mistake of bringing my laptop and had to ask a stranger to look after it since I couldn't bring it in and there were no lockers.

Your visa appointment is like an interview where the person will ask questions about your intent to study a given subject (e.g., "What will you be studying?" "Why are you interested in [field of study]?"). Depending on the person you talk to at the consulate, they may ask you different questions. You may be asked more questions if the U.S. considers your field to be related to national security (e.g., biochemistry).

Checklist to apply for a student visa (check the Department of Homeland Security and your school's website for updates and fill in the blanks with other documents that are relevant for you):

☐ Current passport (Note: must be valid at least six months beyond your period of stay in the U.S.)

☐ All past passports

☐ One color photograph (5cm*5cm) taken within the last six months

☐ I-20 (make sure all information is correct)

☐ Nonimmigrant visa electronic application form (DS-160) confirmation page (you will fill out the application form on the consulate's webpage [the webpage link will be different based on your country of origin])

☐ Receipt of payment for nonimmigrant visa processing fee

☐ SEVIS payment receipt

☐ _____

_____

_____

☐ _____

_____

_____

☐ _____

_____

_____

☐ _____

_____

_____

☐ _____

_____

_____

After reading this chapter, reflect:

- How did you thank yourself for taking the time and energy to apply to schools/programs?

- If you were to apply to more schools/programs in the future, what would you do differently?

- What might you still need to move the visa application forward?

Chapter 5

Planning Ahead: Connecting with current students, securing housing, purchasing textbooks, and making travel plans

This chapter includes:

- Connecting with current international students.

- Securing housing.

- Tips on purchasing textbooks and reading materials.

- Making travel plans.

- Creating a timeline for yourself.

> **To make the most of this chapter, reflect:**
>
> - What information do you already have to prepare for your travels to the U.S.? Such as what do you need to purchase before your trip; information related to what airlines you can take and which airport you're flying into.

Beyond ensuring your passport and visa are in order, there are a number of other things you may want to begin thinking about and doing. Before you start planning, read this entire section so you have a more thorough understanding of what you need to plan for.

Connecting with Current International Students

You may have already connected with other international students during the application process. This is a good time to revisit those contacts and make new ones. Get in touch with your school's international student organizations and the Office of International Services. Consider other groups that may provide support or connect you with students from your home country. For example, I would usually join the Taiwanese Student Association Facebook group. Some student organizations might host informational sessions for new students in their home countries. It may be possible to meet with international students virtually or in person if they happen to be visiting home.

Current students can give advice about what to bring (e.g., what you can buy locally and what you cannot), what to expect (e.g., cultural norms), when to buy a plane ticket, how to purchase a car, how to plan around childcare (e.g., scheduling classes around daycare dropoff and pickup times, finding a babysitter), etc. It can also be helpful to connect with other students going to study abroad and maybe even coordinate travel plans.

What are some questions a current student could answer? What are some organizations or individuals you can connect with? Make a goal to connect with three people/organizational leaders so you can get different perspectives. List them here:

1 _____

_____

2 _____

_____

3 _____

_____

Securing Housing

Most universities require first-year undergraduates to live in an on-campus residence hall. Other students may have more options. I recommend that new students live closer to campus to facilitate participating in campus life and building a sense of belonging. If you live further away, you might need to determine if you can rely on public/communal transportation (provided by the city, school, or your apartment complex) or if you need to buy a car.

Current students can help you learn where to look for housing; international student or other student groups on social media may also be useful sources of information. You may be able to find students looking for roommates or trying to sublet their apartments, which can lower your costs (sometimes substantially, depending on where you are studying). Another consideration is the safety of neighborhoods; you can Google crime rates or get the information from other students. Other ways you can look up housing are websites such as Craigslist. org, apartment.com, etc.

Depending on where the school is located, public transportation may not be convenient. If that is the case, your schedule may be determined by when you can access transportation. Before you consider buying a car, factor in the (in)convenience and additional costs of parking, car registration and insurance, maintenance fees, taxes, etc. If you decide to buy a car, you may find more affordable options in online student groups where current students sell their vehicles.

Purchasing Textbooks and Reading Materials

If you can, find out what classes you will be taking and the required materials. For more information about textbooks, you can visit the school's bookstore website or email your professors for a copy of their syllabus. The international versions of the textbook can be more affordable than buying them in the U.S. My first semester, I purchased the international versions of my textbooks at a third of the price. If you do not plan on lugging your textbooks from home, other affordable options include:

- renting your textbooks from the school's bookstore or Amazon,

- renting or buying e-books or audiobooks,

- borrowing books from the school or public library (Note: there may be a limited number of copies, so you would have to act fast),

- asking if the professor of the class will let you borrow the materials, or

- seeing if the textbook is available in open educational resource databases that your school has purchased.

You can also ask the professor if you can purchase the previous version of the textbook, which tends to be cheaper.

Beyond textbooks, journal articles can often be accessed through your school's library website. A librarian can help you know where and how to search and, if something is unavailable, they may be able to help you gain access to it without paying to unlock it. Many academics will also email you the full text of their articles if you reach out to them directly.

Steps to determine what textbooks and reading materials you will need and where to access them:

1 _____

_____

2 _____

_____

3 _____

_____

Making Travel Plans

Check the Office of International Services' website to learn about the best way to get to the school. Find out where the nearest airports are, if there are shuttles or public transportation available, and if there are specific hours that they operate. It is helpful to do this before purchasing plane tickets because it may impact which airport you choose to fly into or what time you plan to land. If shuttles and public transportation are not available when/where you land, you can see if the international student organization or Office of International Services have volunteers who can pick you up. As a token of appreciation, you can offer to pay for gas or treat them to a meal. You can also plan to travel with another international student so that you can split the cost.

It is recommended that you buy tickets for international flights approximately three months in advance for the best prices and more flight options. You can purchase them on your own or through a travel agency. Remember to allow yourself enough time to go through customs – you need to do this at your first point of entry in the U.S., so if you're taking a connecting flight, be sure your layover is long enough. The lines can be very long and take a few hours. Another thing to note is the distance between customs and the gate for your connecting flight; some airports are quite large and you might have to cover a significant distance. Tip: Be sure to use the restroom once you get off the plane and before you get in line to go through customs.

Make your travel plan:

1 _____

_____

2 _____

_____

3 _____

_____

Timeline

There is A LOT to do before you leave! Create a timeline of what you need to do or purchase. This may include scheduling time to meet with friends before you leave, making appointments for immunization shots and physical examinations, purchasing items you want to bring from home (e.g., stationery, snacks, and hygienic items that may not be readily available in the U.S. [particular brands of hair products, menstrual products, etc.]), and if you have children, researching when to enroll them in schools.

Make a timeline:

1 _____

_____

2 _____

_____

3 _____

_____

After reading this chapter, reflect:

- What information or things do you still need to be prepared for your upcoming travels?

~~Surviving~~ Thriving in the U.S.

In this section of the guide, I provide information about what comes after you arrive in the U.S. I invite you to be proactive and learn about your environment and what resources you can access to not just survive but THRIVE in the U.S.

How to use this section of the book:

- If you just arrived in the U.S., start here: ***Chapter 6: You made it! You're here in the U.S.***

- To better understand the cultural context in the U.S., start here: ***Chapter 7: Learning about U.S. history and culture***

- To reflect on the ways you might change or have already changed since you've been in the U.S., start here: ***Chapter 8: Homesickness, psychological adjustment, and facing discrimination***

- To explore ways to support your health, start here: ***Chapter 9: Attending to your physical, mental, and spiritual health***

- To build new relationships in the U.S. and maintain relationships back home, start here: ***Chapter 10: Building and maintaining your social support***

- To maintain your finances while being mindful of your visa status, start here: ***Chapter 11: Taking care of your financial well-being***

- To benefit from tips for academic success, start here: ***Chapter 12: Thriving in academics***

- To jumpstart your career and move towards your professional goals, start here: ***Chapter 13: Investing in your career***

- To find legal guidance for everyday needs (ex. breaking a lease or dealing with a car accident), start here: ***Chapter 14: Getting legal advice***

- To explore other resources your school provides, start here: ***Chapter 15: Other helpful on-campus resources***

- To identify the resources the surrounding community has to offer, start here: ***Chapter 16: Familiarizing yourself with local and community resources***

- If you feel like you have a good grasp of the resources from the previous sections, start here: ***Chapter 17: Putting it all together and next steps***

Chapter 6

You made it! You're here in the U.S.

This chapter includes:

- Tips for adjusting to the time difference.

- Resources from the Office of International Services.

- What thriving means and how the rest of the book can help you achieve it!

To make the most of this chapter, reflect:

- What are you excited about and looking forward to in the U.S.?

- What are you nervous or worried about when it comes to being in the U.S.?

Now that you've arrived in your new home, it's time to let reality settle in. The first thing you'll need to do is get acclimated to the time difference. This could take a few days or even weeks, depending on the time change from your home country and your own body's adjustment. I would recommend planning ahead and giving yourself ample time to settle in before school starts. Jet lag may leave you feeling fatigued during the day and energetic at night. While you may feel like staying in bed all day, you can adjust more quickly if you are active during the day. Try going to stores to buy essentials or, if you've received your student ID and the school gym is open, going there to exercise.

Once you've had some time to adjust, it's helpful to familiarize yourself with the various resources available to you. Be sure to attend the International Student Orientation, which should provide comprehensive information on maintaining your student visa status (very important!) and other tips about your school and the surrounding community. For example, there may be a church or community organization that helps international students settle in the U.S. by hosting gatherings, giving away donations (e.g., clothes, furniture), or offering rides to grocery stores. To get started, check out the Office of International Services' website for their recommended resources. If the site is useful, bookmark it so that you can refer back to it easily.

As you read on, you'll notice that I don't see academic success as the most important thing; instead, I take a holistic view of your wellness as it relates to culture, psychological, physical, mental, spiritual, relational, and financial domains. Students often struggle with academics when other areas of life are not balanced. You'll be better equipped for academic success if you're well supported, and your needs are being met.

In the following pages, I provide examples from Indiana University Bloomington, where I received my doctoral degree, to give you an idea of the resources that U.S. institutions may offer. This is not an exhaustive list but a guide to help you start being more intentional and strategic about what resources to utilize during your time as an international student.

After reading this chapter, reflect:

- What are some initial resources or information the Office of International Services provides that are pertinent to me?

- Beyond academic success, what areas in my life should I attend to while I am in the U.S.?

Chapter 7

Learning about U.S. History and Culture

This chapter includes:

- Why it is important to learn about U.S. history and culture.

- How to learn about U.S. history and culture.

To make the most of this chapter, reflect:

- What do I already know about U.S. history and culture?

- Are the sources I learned from reliable?

A lot of international students that I've talked to, including my clients and research participants, feel like they are just here to be students. As foreigners in the U.S., they do not feel the need to be concerned with what is happening in U.S. politics, culture, big events, social movements, etc. I would like to challenge that idea. It is crucial that you are educated at least on the policies that are directly related to you. One obvious way that current politics could impact you is through ever-changing immigration policies. Further, even as an international student, you are entering into an existing system. Given that U.S. history is built upon oppressing people with marginalized identities (e.g., people of color, LGBTQ folks), it is important to recognize your role in the existing system (e.g., how you benefit from it and how you are marginalized).

I would also recommend that you attend a few events hosted by your school's Multicultural Center to learn more about U.S. history and culture from the perspective of people who are not always represented or misrepresented in Hollywood movies or mainstream media. These perspectives are not always taught in the classroom and without them, you would be missing out on the American experience, which is very diverse. Every month is an awareness month for a different culture, identity, or presenting issue. Often, there will be related events featured across campus. While educating yourself on history is useful, it is equally important to learn from the people you see today. You should also be aware of social movements in the U.S., your school, the community outside of your school, in your field, or even in your program. For example, the national and global Black Lives Matter movement has impacts at the university and program levels. Sometimes these movements may rise to the global level and even impact the relationship between your home country and the U.S.

You may come from a country/place that frowns, culturally or even legally, upon speaking against the mainstream narrative. It can be useful to pause and reflect on any resistance coming from within, such as "Why am I having such a strong reaction to information related to politics?" Don't be dismissive of your reactions; they may be self-protective since speaking up can result in threats to your physical safety in some places/cultures. I would encourage you to remain curious and try to put aside any judgmental thoughts that are coming up.

Name three resources and/or events on your campus to help you learn about history and different cultures in the U.S.:

Example:

I will attend two events hosted by the Neal-Marshall Black Culture Center (275 N. Jordan Ave, Bloomington, IN 47405) during the month of February, which is Black History Month.

1 _____

_____

2 _____

_____

3 _____

_____

After reading this chapter, reflect:

- What are some social movements going on globally, in the U.S., in your state, your school, your program, or your community?

- What are you interested in learning more about?

- Where can you find more information?

Chapter 8

Homesickness, Psychological Adjustment, and Facing Discrimination

This chapter includes:

- Recognizing and coping with homesickness.

- Noticing how you adjust to a new environment and the identity shifts that may come with the process.

- Handling discrimination and stereotypes.

To make the most of this chapter, reflect:

- What are you having a difficult time adjusting to in the U.S.? What do you miss from home?

- Which of your strengths or characteristics have helped you adjust to the U.S. so far?

- What aspects of your identity have you thought about more or differently in your time in the U.S.?

- What is your experience when you encounter people who are different from you or what you are accustomed to?

Homesickness

Some research has shown that, on average, international students start to experience homesickness in their third month in the U.S. Given that this is an average, some may experience it sooner and others later. Some people may miss the food from their home country, while others may feel guilty for missing out on the lives of their loved ones while they are abroad.

Researchers have developed a cross-cultural loss scale (Wang et al., 2015) that speaks to some of the tangible and psychological losses that international students experience when they are in the U.S. It is important to know that you are not the only one experiencing homesickness and feelings of loss.[8]

Whether this is your first week or third year in the U.S., take a moment to list the things you miss about home. It's also okay to list things that others may consider minor; this is about your own feelings and experience.

1 _____

_____

2 _____

_____

3 _____

_____

---

[8] To learn more about the study and the items on the scale, check out: Wang, K. T., Wei, M., Zhao, R., Chuang, C. C., & Li, F. (2015). The Cross-Cultural Loss Scale: Development and psychometric evaluation. *Psychological Assessment, 27*(1), 42-53.

4 _____

_____

5 _____

_____

To cope with homesickness, some people learn to cook traditional foods that remind them of home or choose to be more intentional about social media, so they are not constantly exposing themselves to the feeling of missing out.

Write down ways that you have been dealing with what you miss from home.

1 _____

_____

2 _____

_____

3 _____

_____

4 _____

_____

5 _____

_____

Reread what you just wrote and consider whether the coping strategies work most of the time. There are no perfect solutions, which is why I emphasize most of the time. If the strategies work less than half of the time, brainstorm more effective ways to cope. For example, if you're scrolling through social media to stay connected to family and friends back home, but it makes you feel worse, you may want to schedule phone or video calls with the people you miss instead.

Psychological Adjustment and Identity Shifts

In the model of adjustment and adaptation, scholars break down the reasons (e.g., English ability, cultural empathy, open-mindedness) that could impact adjustment in different areas (academic, sociocultural, and psychological).[9] The model may be useful to examine how you are adapting and how you can make slight adjustments to manage your new life in the U.S. When I first came to the U.S., I constantly compared the Taiwanese food here to the food back home. I was coming in with a certain standard and setting myself up for disappointment instead of appreciating the food as it was. I still catch myself doing it now, but I remind myself to keep an open mind and to be curious to try new things.

A key component to adjustment is social support. When considering adjustment and adaptation, you may have heard of the terms *acculturation* and *enculturation*. The former means adopting the dominant culture (in this case, the U.S. white culture) and the latter means adopting your ethnic culture. Researchers discusses four strategies used when folks migrate to a different country/culture: integration (bicultural), assimilation, separation, and marginalization. Integration is considered the successful strategy because individuals adopt values and traditions from both cultures (acculturation and enculturation). Assimilation means that the individual primarily adopts the dominant culture (high acculturation and low enculturation). Separation is when individuals mostly identify with their own ethnic heritage (low acculturation and high enculturation). Lastly, marginalization is when folks reject dominant culture as well as their ethnic heritage (low acculturation and enculturation).[10] These different strategies can be seen in how you seek out social support. A key component of the adjustment and adaptation model is strengthening your social support. Do you have American friends or international friends from other countries? Do you form community with people from your home country? Do you keep to yourself? For more tips on social support, see Chapter 10 on Building and Maintaining Your Social Support.

As you adjust, adapt, acculturate, and enculturate, you may notice a shift in your identities and how you see the world. This is perfectly normal; it's actually quite common. Friends and family in your home country might comment that you are "becoming American." You might start to disagree with how some things are done back in your home country. For in

---

9   Read more here: Schartner, A., & Young, T. J. (2016) Towards an integrated conceptual model of international student adjustment and adaptation. *European Journal of Higher Education, 6*(4), 372-386.

10   Read more here: Berry, J. W. (1994). Acculturation and psychological adaptation. In A.-M. Bouvy, F. J. R. van de Vijver, P. Boski, & P. Schmitz (Eds.), *Journeys into cross cultural psychology* (pp. 129–141). Swets & Zeitlinger.

stance, Taiwanese people are known to be easygoing, and I used to pride myself on how many people complimented me on my friendliness. Being in the U.S. for over a decade now, I have learned to set healthy boundaries by being more direct about things that I am uncomfortable with. A few years ago, I finally told my mother that I did not appreciate her constant comments about my physique and weight. We were both surprised by my sudden firmness, but she apologized for making me feel like the way I looked was more important than my personality or academic accomplishments. She promised to try to stop. Over the last few years, there were times when she slipped into her old ways, but when I gently reminded her, she was able to respect my boundary.

As your identities shift, you may learn more about yourself and become more aware of social issues. For example, when the start of the COVID-19 pandemic precipitated an uptick in Asian hate crimes, I found myself thinking more about being Asian and wondering how non-Asians perceived me. To better understand the context behind various social issues, you can attend multicultural events or do your own research. While you are doing research, be sure to cross-reference between reliable sources so that you are not consuming misinformation. To find credible sources, you can examine the author's credentials and affiliations, investigate the references cited by the author, make sure the source is up-to-date, and check the reputation of the publisher/platform and the endorsements it has received.

If you are coming from a country that is more conservative than the U.S., you may experience more freedom and autonomy in terms of freedom of speech and how you present yourself. During my internship at The Ohio State University, I co-facilitated an international LGBTQ group. I worked with new students on celebrating their new found freedom and graduating students on pre-grieving the loss of being "out" and potentially having to "go back in the closet" when they returned home, due to concerns for their safety.

For others, you might encounter race differently in the U.S. given the country's unique racial history. You might notice that on almost every official form, one of the first questions is what race(s) you identify with. As with the adjustment models I mentioned earlier, there is also a model that was developed for international students of color on how their racial identity emerges in the U.S.[11]

Discrimination and Stereotypes

Discrimination and stereotypes are often related to how others perceive your social identities (e.g., race, ethnicity, gender, sexual orientation, socioeconomic status, religion, spirituality) based on your appearance, demeanor, accent, etc. Due to the model minority

---

[11] Read more here: Fries-Britt, S., Mwangi, C. A. G., & Peralta, A. M. (2014). Learning race in a U.S. context: An emergent framework on the perceptions of race among foreign-born students. *Journal of Diversity in Higher Education, 7*(1), 1–13.

myth, international students, especially those coming from Asian[12] and African[13] countries, are often held to a higher standard, which can lead to more academic stress. If you experience discrimination, it is entirely up to you what actions you decide to take. First, you can do nothing. This is a valid response and you do not need to justify why you would rather not do anything about it. If you would like to take action, be sure to ensure your own physical and psychological safety first. You can also directly address the person who is discriminating against you. For example, if someone refuses to serve you at a restaurant, you can let them know that it is your right to dine there, or you can ask to see their manager. Finally, you can delegate by letting your friends know how you would like them to intervene (or not) if someone discriminates against you.

Additionally, most universities have reporting systems, including anonymous reporting and filing an official complaint. Depending on your school, these reports can be handled by different offices, sometimes it is the Dean of Students Office, campus police, or other entities. You may also seek mental health counseling to talk to someone in a confidential setting (see the next chapter on Attending to Your Physical, Mental, and Spiritual Health).

After reading this chapter, reflect:

- What in this chapter resonated with you?

- What ways of adjusting do you want to continue and what would you like to tweak?

- How can you learn more about the different aspects of your identity?

---

12   Read more here: Walton, J., & Truong, M. (2023). A review of the model minority myth: Understanding the social, educational and health impacts. *Ethnic & Racial Studies, 46*(3), 391-419.
13   Read more here: Ukpokodu, O. N. (2018). African immigrants, the "New Model Minority": Examining the reality in US K-12 schools. *The Urban Review, 50*, 69-96.

Chapter 9

Attending to Your Physical, Mental, and Spiritual Health

This chapter includes:

- Navigating U.S. health insurance and institutions.

- Attending to your physical health, exercise, and nutrition.

- Caring for your mental and emotional health.

- Building community to uplift your spiritual health.

To make the most of this chapter, reflect:

- How are you taking care of your physical, mental, and spiritual health currently?

Navigating Health Insurance and Institutions

As an international student, you are usually required to have health insurance. If you are able, I would encourage you to purchase the insurance that your school offers because private insurance may not meet your school's requirements. With the mandatory student fees, international students are eligible to utilize the student health center on campus (if the school has one). Some student health centers accept student health insurance and/or other health insurance for some of their services. With health insurance, you can also access other medical facilities off campus. Be mindful that some cities have a few predominant insurance companies that allow for more affordable access to healthcare. Depending on the insurance policy, the co-pay (fees you pay directly, which are not covered by insurance) can range from $0 (usually for preventative visits, such as flu shots or consultation appointments) to $20 or $30 (sometimes more) per visit. Be mindful of deductibles (your out-of-pocket amount before your insurance pays) and co-insurance (the percentage of how much you pay for services). Every school offers different health services. To determine if the school's insurance is a good fit for you, be sure to read what it covers, especially if you have health needs that require special treatment or medication. If you have questions about the school's health insurance or if your private insurance is sufficient, reach out to the Office of International Services.

Navigating insurance and the U.S. healthcare system can be tricky! Even after taking courses on the U.S. healthcare system as part of my public health minor, I am still often very confused. Make sure you have your insurance card, which will have some basic information on the front, such as your insurance ID number, group ID number, and various co-pays for different services. On the back of the insurance card, there are usually different customer service numbers you can call. Sometimes international students would rather try to find the information themselves than make a phone call, however, it can be easier to call and ask a question. For example, during the COVID-19 pandemic, my insurance waived co-pays for virtual visits with my therapist and some medical appointments. They kept extending the date, yet this information was not readily available to me or my therapist. I called my insurance's behavioral health customer service line (it is a separate number from general customer service) to inquire about the copays and I had to call back four or five times as the deadline was extended further. Luckily, my insurance does not have a complicated phone tree, so I was able to get my question answered quickly. Insurance customer service can also let you know if a healthcare provider is within or outside of your network (whether the doctor takes your insurance or not). The same service can be vastly more expensive if the provider is outside of your network (sometimes you can submit receipts and request reimbursement from your insurance). Depending on the type of insurance you have, you might need a referral from your primary care provider in order to see a specialist. Your insurance might also have a limit on the number of sessions that are covered for physical therapy and alternative medicine (e.g., acupuncture, chiropractor).

Physical Health, Exercise, and Nutrition

Regular exercise not only improves physical health but improves concentration and boosts mental health and memory. As most cities in the U.S. are designed for driving and have limited functional sidewalks, you will need to be intentional about remaining active. I encourage you to set up a workout routine for yourself. For some of you that might mean following a yoga instructor on YouTube, for others that might be going to group exercise classes and using the weight room at the recreational center. Fortunately, as a student at your school, you will likely have access to the campus gym. Sometimes the campus gym will offer affordable personal trainers to assist you in using the equipment and achieving your fitness goals. While the goal of having an exercise routine is to maintain an active/healthy body, it is also important to rest when you are tired and to ensure you keep your body adequately fueled.

The food in the U.S. may be different from what you are used to, so you may need to take some time to figure out how to maintain a balanced diet. A dietitian may be able to help you brainstorm what local foods you can substitute for the foods you ate back home. You may be able to access the support of a dietitian on campus or through the doctor's office. Depending on where you study and your transportation, it may be hard to access fresh food. You can research how to access the food you need. For example, there are many food and grocery delivery services in the U.S. Some schools may have farms and gardens where you can receive fresh food for free or purchase it at a relatively low price. You can also subscribe to community-supported agriculture (CSA) which provides you with in-season vegetables, fruits, and sometimes meat.

Finally, you may have noticed that beauty standards in the U.S. include a toned body for all genders, which is not a realistic expectation for everyone. If you become overly worried about your body image, engage in excessive amounts of exercise, limit your food intake (including skipping meals), or overeat, it may be a sign to seek help (see the following section on Mental and Emotional Health for information on counseling centers).

Mental and Emotional Health

I recommend you take advantage of the campus counseling center to help with your transition into U.S. culture. Counseling centers typically offer individual counseling, group counseling, and workshops. Some centers may even have therapists who speak multiple languages. If this is something you might want to check out, make an appointment sooner than later. Counseling centers become busier as the semester goes on (student stress levels are directly related to the point in the semester); if you try to book an appointment later in the semester, you might find yourself waiting several weeks before you can see the next available therapist. It's also fine to give it a try and see which therapist you work well with, or even decide therapy is not for you at this point in time. Group counseling is also a great way to receive social support. Some counseling centers offer identity-based groups, such as international student groups, which can be especially helpful for discussing shared experiences and empowering each other.

College counseling centers usually operate on what is called the "short-term model," which means that in order to serve as many students as they can, students have a limited number of sessions they can utilize. Instead of weekly sessions, sessions are typically spaced a few weeks apart. Counseling centers are also typically training sites for master's or doctoral students studying to become mental health providers, so don't be surprised if your clinician introduces themselves as a trainee who is supervised by a professional staff member. If you know that you might want to see a therapist more frequently/for longer, you can ask the counseling center staff to provide you with a referral to a community provider. Be sure to let them know if you have any preferences for the therapist, such as their gender, race, international background, languages spoken, therapeutic style, etc. If you decide to see a community provider, be sure to check if the provider is within-network; if not, ask your insurance (the behavioral health number on the back of the insurance card) if they can reimburse you for an out-of-network provider, up to what percentage/dollar amount, and how to submit claims.

Mental health counseling in the U.S. is bound by confidentiality. Most things you discuss are considered confidential; however, there are some limits to confidentiality, such as if you disclose imminent danger to yourself or others, or if you disclose suspected abuse or neglect of children, elderly folks, or people with a disability. In these instances, the provider should notify you that they need to break confidentiality in order to protect those involved. If you have questions about such protocols, you can ask your provider to explain them to you. Depending on which discipline the therapist is in, they also abide by the related state laws and professional ethics. For example, I am licensed as a psychologist in the state of Pennsylvania, this means that I can only see clients who are physically located in the state and need to adhere to the laws of Pennsylvania and the professional ethics of the American Psychological Association.

When you first meet with a mental health provider, whether it is a brief consultation or intake session, you can ask questions to assess for fit:

- Any questions that you have about confidentiality and its limits.

- Does the provider take your insurance? If not, can they provide statements for you to submit for reimbursement with your insurance?

- Questions about how the provider typically works with clients:

  - What is the provider's therapeutic style?

  - What is the recommended frequency of sessions (e.g., weekly, biweekly)?

  - Anything else you're curious about that you've read about the provider on their website.

  - Has the provider ever worked with international students (or other socio-cultural identities that are important to you, e.g., LGBTQ+)?

  - Does the provider handle crisis? What is their crisis protocol?

  - Do they typically see clients in-person, telehealth, or hybrid?

  - How does the provider assess for when you have reached your therapy goals?

  - What is the provider's cancellation policy? Are there any late cancellation/rescheduling fees?

You can also share anything you'd like the provider to know about you.

While you are in counseling, it's also okay to give your provider feedback so that they can better serve you (e.g., "I would like to focus on x issue instead of y," "I would like to learn more coping strategies instead of talking about my feelings.").

Remember, don't wait until things are really bad to reach out for help.

Gather as much detail as you can about the Health Center, Counseling Center, and/or other physical and mental health facilities you might utilize during your stay in the U.S.:

Example:

The Counseling and Psychological Services is located in the Health Center (600 N Jordan Ave, Bloomington, IN 47405). Their hours are Mondays through Fridays from x:xx to x:xx, I can schedule virtual appointments on their website.

_____

_____

_____

_____

_____

_____

You may also be eligible for a few free counseling sessions each year through your student health benefits or, if you are a graduate assistant, the Employee Assistance Program (EAP). Look into whether this support is available to you.

Another resource is the 24/7 (24 hours, 7 days a week) National Suicide Prevention and Crisis Lifeline: 988 and suicidepreventionlifeline.org which enables callers in crisis or distress to talk to someone confidentially. Add this number to your cellphone so that you have it if you, or a friend, needs it. This can be especially helpful when you are having difficulty getting ahold of friends or family and/or do not want to worry those close to you. Some cities or schools offer "warmlines" or peer support. Unlike hotlines, these resources are usually for people who are not in a crisis but would benefit from talking to someone to problem-solve.

Name warmlines or peer support that are available in your area:

_____

_____

_____

Remember, even if you do not need these resources right now, if you are ever in need, you will know exactly where to find them.

Spiritual Health

For some students, it is very important to keep up with their faith and build a community around shared religious/spiritual practices. While some folks may choose to connect virtually with their communities back home, some may join a local community in the U.S. There may be faith communities to explore on campus, in town, or in neighboring places. If you are having trouble finding a local option, you may be able to find an online resource from a nearby community; the COVID-19 pandemic spurred many religious centers to make their resources available online.

List religious/spiritual communities to connect with in the next few weeks:

_____

_____

_____

_____

After reading this chapter, reflect:

- In terms of physical, mental, and spiritual health, what are you doing well and what do you need to change to balance your wellness?

Chapter 10
Building and Maintaining Your Social Support

This chapter includes:

- How to find and build community in the U.S.

- Ways to maintain and prioritize relationships in your home country.

- Developing relationships with Americans and managing expectations.

- Dating and setting boundaries in the U.S.

To make the most of this chapter, reflect:

- Who do you consider part of your community, both in the U.S. and in your home country?

- What are your needs and expectations? Are they being met by your existing social support network?

- What types of relationships would you like to have?

Starting your life in a new country is not the easiest thing to do. While technology allows you to stay in contact with friends and family back home, they may not always understand your experiences. International students often report that they only talk about the positive things, so that their family doesn't worry. While it might seem easier not to share, keeping challenges to yourself can take a toll and lead to feelings of isolation.

Research has shown the importance of building a community that lifts you up. As mentioned before, it can be helpful to live closer to campus so that you can attend events (e.g., movie or game nights, socials, happy hours). Even if you are a graduate student, you can still enjoy the diverse student organizations that American schools offer. Try to connect with people beyond those from your home country or area of study. As you continue to build your network, including people from diverse backgrounds can help bring new perspectives and limit drama that may arise in insular communities.

For international students who have brought their children with them, it can be helpful to consider how to balance your roles as student and as parent (e.g., asking professors for accommodations in order to attend your children's parent-teacher conference; meeting other international student parents to form a community for childcare).

Name three student organizations and/or communities of interest and how you will reach out:

Example:

Taiwanese Student Association. I will join their Facebook group and attend their Moon Festival event.

1 _____

_____

2 _____

_____

3 _____

_____

Maintaining Relationships from Back Home

In the course of my research on how international students' parents support them, I noticed that there were very few studies focused on how international students maintained their relationships from home. It almost seemed like there was an assumption that international students lost all their home connections and depended exclusively on the support they built in the U.S. This is both untrue and unrealistic.

Envision how you want your relationships with your loved ones back home to look. It might also be helpful to discuss their expectations for the relationship. In doing so, you can negotiate and create a realistic plan to maintain the relationships that matter to you. For example, the time difference may make it harder to have a daily Skype session with your best friend. Scheduling specific times to talk might lessen your stress (or guilt) about trying to keep up with school AND relationships. When I first came to the U.S., my mother expected me to call her frequently because it was my first time living on my own and in another country. To develop my autonomy and independence without worrying her, I assured her that "no news is good news" and discussed how frequently I would like to call. Luckily, she was understanding of my expectations and boundaries.

International students often feel guilty for missing out on important milestones, like new jobs, weddings, births, and funerals. This feeling can arise or be heightened when you scroll through social media and see life updates from your friends back home. Rather than pushing those feelings away, it's important to acknowledge them so you can start to find alternative ways to share in important events.

Think of three people or groups from home who you would like to keep in contact with. Consider the type of relationship you want to have with each of them and come up with a plan to maintain the closeness you desire.

1 _____

_____

2 _____

_____

3 _____

_____

Developing Relationships with Americans

This topic is always popular with international students in my workshops. Those who want to study in a different country are often genuinely interested in immersing themselves in a different culture, which includes meeting locals.

For many of us, much of what we know about Americans is shaped by the American music we listen to or Hollywood movies — and we only get to see certain blockbuster movies in other countries. While some of it may be true (e.g., Americans value autonomy and independence), those portrayals are limited. There are many regional, cultural, and individual differences and you want to avoid stereotyping others, just as you would not want to be stereotyped.

On-campus events that are dedicated to cross-cultural exchange make it easy for all parties involved. Language exchanges, international friendships, host families, and cultural hours create opportunities for international students to become more integrated into the community and to make connections with Americans. These events are usually co-sponsored by the Office of International Services or a community organization that is international-friendly. When I first came to the U.S. for my master's degree, I signed up for language exchange partners and didn't realize I had signed up with four different organizations. I ended up getting to know four different American women! One lent me medieval costumes, braided my hair, and took me to a Renaissance Festival in her hometown. Another went to a campus cultural hour with me where we participated in games and activities.

Back home, I never went to anything on my own; I always had a friend or two by my side. In the U.S., I found it helpful to attend events alone to keep myself from relying on a familiar friend and to push me to reach out to strangers. Striking out on your own takes some courage but it can also be very rewarding. Once I challenged myself to be more independent, I was able to recognize and befriend others who also went to the events by themselves. For me, it is much easier to approach individual people than those who are in groups.

Beyond the initial difficulty of making friends, you need to build and maintain those friendships. A difference that shocked me in the U.S. was how people canceled plans at the last minute. The term "flakey" describes people who are unreliable; in this case, people who do not show up when they say they will. Initially, I took this very personally, interpreting it as being about me and feeling rejected. Back home, people took other people's times very seriously and never canceled, unless there was an emergency. To deal with this unexpected level of flakiness, I set boundaries. I gave people the benefit of the doubt up to three times. If they flaked on me three times, I protected my time by waiting for them to reach out, instead of being proactive. I realized that dependability was a significant relationship value for me — I needed my friends to show up for me, literally and metaphorically. My lasting friendships were with American friends who shared these values. It is important to note that if you behave this way (canceling plans last minute), Americans might also be surprised and/or offended.

It's okay to be sad or disappointed about friendships that don't work out. There are a lot of reasons friendships end and I've had my fair share of grief. Sometimes a friend graduates and moves away; if you're in a doctoral program, you'll say goodbye to a lot of folks whose programs are shorter. Sometimes you move away, leaving folks behind. Sometimes you are in the same place but because of flakiness or another reason it doesn't work out. The process of making and keeping friends can come with positive and negative emotions. Talk to your friends and maybe even a counselor to explore your thoughts, feelings, and reactions.

Ultimately, as my Chilean friend said, you make friends in the U.S. "the same way you make friends anywhere: with a combination of being outgoing and genuinely interested in what people have to say." Good luck!

Dating in the U.S.

Another aspect of U.S. social life that was different than what I was used to in Taiwan was the dating scene.

Growing up back home, people were either friends or boyfriends/girlfriends/romantic partners. There was no in-between. However, there is an in-between in the U.S. It is called dating. Dating is a stage when people are not officially in a relationship but are trying to figure out if they want to be. Some people prefer to be monogamous (only dating one person at a time) while others may date multiple partners (this may also be the case in official relationships, which is called polyamory). During this stage, people may go on dates that usually involve some kind of activity, such as dinners, movies, and walks. You might have seen these activities reflected in Hollywood movies and American TV shows. Whether you are officially in a relationship or not, it is always helpful to communicate expectations to your partner(s) to minimize misunderstandings and assumptions.

In the U.S., there are many different dating apps including Tinder, OK Cupid, Hinge, Bumble, and Coffee Meets Bagel. Some apps are made for particular populations, such as East Meets East (Asian people), Grindr (LGBTQ+ community, mostly gay and queer men), and Christian Mingle (Christian folks). If you decide to use an online dating platform, make sure you are comfortable with it by observing the culture of the app. For example, some apps are known for finding hookups/one nightstands (sexual encounters with strangers), rather than relationships, and if your goal is to find the latter, those apps may not be a good fit.

Another thing that was quite different for me was the hookup culture in the U.S. It is important to note that in the U.S., college is a time for people to explore their identities, such as gender and sexual orientation. There may be more openness to having sexual contact (e.g., kissing, touching, penetration) without a romantic relationship than you are accustomed to. Hollywood movies and American shows also portray sexual contact more casually than entertainment produced in some other countries. It is important to keep in mind, however, that there is a range in how individual Americans feel about such behavior. To protect yourself and your partner(s), it is important to have an open dialogue about sexual health, which could include requesting information on one another's history of sexually transmitted diseases (STDs) or sexually transmitted infections (STIs) and getting tested (these tests are usually covered through health insurance). To learn more about sexual health and/or access free condoms or other contraception, you can visit your school's Women's Center, LGBTQ Resource Center, Relationship and Sexual Violence Prevention Center, or Health Center.

For any kind of intimacy, it is important to ask for and receive consent (agreement) from all parties involved. Consent is given in the moment and can be taken back anytime; giving consent once does not imply consent in the future, further, someone can stop consenting during the course of sexual activity. For example, consenting to kissing does not mean consenting to touching. If someone is making you uncomfortable, it is okay to say "no" and "stop." While I understand that you may feel embarrassed to express discomfort or fear embarrassing or upsetting the other person, I want to encourage you to assert your boundaries. On the receiving end, if someone tells you "no," "stop," or they seem like they are unresponsive and unable to say "yes," be sure to respect their wishes and boundaries, and avoid making assumptions. Silence should not be assumed to imply consent. If someone is under the influence of drugs or alcohol (note that the legal drinking age is 21 in the U.S.), they are unable to give consent.

List three resources you can utilize for intimate relationships and sexual health and explain what each of them provides:

1 _____

_____

2 _____

_____

3 _____

_____

After reading this chapter, reflect:

- Are you satisfied with your current relationships and social support?

- What can you do to move your current or future relationships in the direction you would like?

Chapter 11

Taking Care of Your Financial Well-Being

This chapter includes:

- Legal income sources for international students.

- Types of on-campus jobs.

- Credit and why it is important to begin building it.

- Educating yourself about CPT and OPT.

- Learning about H1B visas and green cards to understand your options upon graduation.

- Taxes and residential status changes that apply to international students.

- Additional resources to learn more about financial wellness.

> **To make the most of this chapter, reflect:**
>
> - How would you describe your relationship with finances?
>
> - How is your visa tied to your finances, both now and in the future?

It is critical to pay attention to this section so that you do not jeopardize your student visa status. There are different regulations for different types of visas (e.g., J-1, F-1) in terms of whether and how you can earn an income. Although the regulations are relatively stable, it is still important to check to make sure you abide by the rules. All this information should be available on your campus's Office of International Services' website. Below are a few items that I'd recommend you read more than once. Please note that this guide does NOT offer legal or financial advice, so be sure to double-check with your Office of International Services for accuracy and updated changes to policies.

Income Source

Where you receive your income in the U.S. matters! It may be appealing to work at a restaurant and be paid in cash, but I would advise you to think twice. It is against the law for international students to earn income off-campus (see next section on what counts as on-campus employment) and you will likely be on edge while you work. I had a colleague who worked off-campus at a restaurant and their professor came in to dine. The professor later threatened my colleague that if they did not quit their job at the restaurant, the professor would report them to the authorities. Is it worth the few extra dollars to risk being unable to finish your degree or being deported after all the hard work you put in to get to where you are now? This is not to say that money is not important, but you should consider positions that will not jeopardize your education or visa status.

On-Campus Jobs

On-campus jobs refer to work where your employer is the school, whether you are physically on campus or not. F-1 and J-1 student visa holders can work up to 20 hours per week during fall and spring semesters and up to 40 hours per week during the summer semester and other breaks. Be mindful that you may not be eligible for another job if you already hold a graduate assistantship.

Common on-campus jobs include working at the dining halls, bookstore, libraries, and recreation center/gym. Other more niche jobs may require additional training or qualifications; these include working as a student career specialist at the career center or a group exercise instructor at the recreation center. Some of these jobs may be posted on the school or center-specific websites, under a tab called employment /careers/work with us. Other jobs may be found through word of mouth; networking can help you access information that is not readily available on the internet.

If you are interested in on-campus employment, name three employers and when you would need to apply:

1 _____

_____

2 _____

_____

3 _____

_____

Credit

Credit refers to the trust that banks have that you will repay them if they lend you money. This is usually reflected in something called a credit score. Credit scores range between 300-850, with 380-669 considered *fair*, 670-739 *good*, 740-799 *very good*, and >800 *excellent*. Having good credit can help you take out loans for big purchases (e.g., buying a car or house). I suggest you start building credit when you get to the U.S. I was only able to apply for my first credit card after holding an active U.S. bank account and using my debit card responsibly for a year. There are lots of resources online that provide information about how to maintain your credit score, how to determine which credit card(s) meet your needs, etc. Remember to do research when it comes to anything that might impact your credit (e.g., anytime you apply for a new credit card, your credit score will go down because the credit card company conducts a "hard inquiry" on your credit history). Be very mindful of how much debt you take on and plan out your payments, especially if the interest rate is high. Whenever possible, be sure to pay off the entire statement balance so you don't accrue interest.

Some schools have an office dedicated to financial wellness, such as MoneySmarts at Indiana University. I would highly recommend utilizing these offices to help you consider your financial status and ways to improve it.

Applying for CPT and OPT

Your Office of International Services should have regular workshops or host information on its website about CPT (curricular practical training) and OPT (optional practical training). CPT is what you apply for while you are still in school and would like to do a paid internship off-campus; OPT is temporary employment for a year (or three years if you are in a STEM major) upon graduation. I suggest you become familiar with CPT and OPT, in case you might want to apply for them. The timing to apply is crucial and you do not want to miss the window. You may find that you're often more knowledgeable about visa issues than your advisor or employer. You will need to be diligent in keeping up with the laws and regulations so that your visa status is not at risk. For example, I completed a yearlong full-time internship while on CPT and I had to inform my employer that in order to qualify to apply for OPT upon graduation, I could not work more than 365 days. My employer was able to reduce my internship length to 364 days.

List how to apply for CPT and OPT at your school:

To apply to CPT, I need _____

_____

_____

To apply to OPT, I need _____

_____

_____

Passive Income

For international students, there are only a few legal ways to earn passive income. You are allowed to invest in stocks and real estate. For example, some international students might purchase a house or apartment, stay there during their studies, and sell it when they graduate. You are also allowed to receive prize money from competitions that are not on campus. However, you are not allowed to make money from your own company or from the royalties of publishing a book in the U.S. If you were to do so, you would have to donate all your earnings from the company or royalties. You may publish a book in other countries and earn your royalties that way.

H1B Visa and Green Card

You may have heard people talk about the H1B visa and green card. These types of immigration statuses are related to employment, although the latter could also be acquired through marriage with an American citizen. As you're job searching and interviewing, it would be helpful to know if employers have hired other international workers and sponsored H1B visas[14] and green cards.

International workers can remain in the U.S. for up to six years on a series of H1B visas and one H1B visa can last up to three years. One of my colleagues received her first H1B visa for a single year and it was quite stressful to have to prepare all the paperwork again in such a short period of time. You can also have concurrent H1B visas sponsored by different employers, with one being the main employer (you will need to negotiate with your employers about how you will split your time). A lot of the restrictions that apply to J-1 and F-1 student visas regarding income sources (e.g., stocks and real estate) also apply to the H1B visa. Note at the time of this writing: it is illegal for employers to request that the employee pay the lawyer fees regarding H1B visas.

For an employment-based green card, you would want to start advocating for it as soon as you can after receiving your H1B, as it can take anywhere from four months to years before your application is approved, depending on your nationality (currently there is a backlog of applications for folks from China and India) and the track of your green card application. Your employer will typically have you work with an immigration lawyer. There are different employment-based "preference immigrant" categories and the lawyer may have suggestions on which you would qualify for. A benefit for your employer is that if they begin your green card petition within 15 months of your hire, they do not need to go through the labor certification process (i.e., open up your position and go through another round of interviews),

---

14   e.g., https://h1bgrader.com/

which can save them money. This can also fast-track your application, buying you more time for the processing of a green card.

Another option is to hire an immigration lawyer to self-sponsor a green card. When you are looking for immigration lawyers, some folks may provide free consultation services for you to ask questions while others may charge you by the hour. EB-1 and EB-2 NIW (National Interest Waiver) are categories for self-sponsorship, typically if you have a graduate or professional degree and some significant contributions to the field (EB-1 has more stringent requirements). In addition, you may be able to apply for self-sponsorship as a graduate student. Sometimes there are external circumstances that may impact this process. For example, because of the COVID-19 pandemic, there is a National Interest Waiver for foreign healthcare professionals to apply for green cards. Given the complexities of the different types of applications, be sure to do your homework and consult with a professional familiar with immigration policies. Immigration lawyers can charge between $100-600/hour so be sure to ask around and get a referral.

Taxes and Residential Status Changes

As an international student, you will have to report your taxes to the U.S. government annually, even if you are not earning an income (Form 8843). Taxes are typically due in mid-April (the exact date may change from year to year). Some universities have volunteers who help international students file taxes their first year. Be aware that your filing status will change from nonresident alien to resident alien after being in the U.S. for more than 3 years (for tax purposes, you will need to calculate the number of calendar days that you are physically in the U.S. to see if your filing status has changed).

Additional Resources

Additional resources can be accessed as books, e-books, or audiobooks at your local library. One recommendation is *Get Good with Money*, by Tiffany "the Budgetnista" Aliche, which discusses financial wholeness in day-to-day language.

After reading this chapter, reflect:

- What do you need to learn more about when it comes to your visa and finances?

- In addition to the resources mentioned in the chapter, where can you learn more or who can you reach out to with questions?

- What is your next financial step given where you are in your schooling?

Chapter 12

Thriving in Academics

This chapter includes:

- The role of your academic advisor.

- Utilizing office hours.

- Differentiating between academic coaching, tutoring, writing center, and disability services, and knowing who to ask for help.

- Tips on studying and engaging in the classroom.

- Knowing what is "good enough."

- Additional resources.

To make the most of this chapter, reflect:

- How are you doing academically — overall and in each course?

- If you are struggling, is it just an academic issue or are you stressed or out of balance in other areas (e.g., physically, emotionally, mentally, spiritually, relationally, financially)?

Academic Advisor

Knowing when and who to ask for help is one of the key elements of success. You will be assigned to an academic advisor; try to meet with them as soon as possible. If a meeting is not possible, send them an email to introduce yourself. Beyond coordinating with them to register for courses each semester, I recommend having regular contact (at least 2-3 times a semester), since they may be helpful to your academic and professional career.

Office Hours

Office hours are another key resource. Office hours are specific times that professors or teaching assistants (TAs) set aside to meet with students. You can also request to meet at other times if you have a scheduling conflict. Office hours are a great way to get to know your professors (this is especially helpful when you are in a big lecture hall class) and ask more detailed questions. Some professors offer resources or opportunities that you may not be aware of otherwise. If you are interested in entering a professor's field, they can give you guidance and more information on how to do so.

Different Academic Services and Knowing Who to Ask for Help

- Academic coaching (note: academic advising is focused on helping you choose/schedule classes based on your major, whereas coaching assists with the process of academic goal setting and achievement),

- Tutoring (this may be subject-specific),

- Writing center (may help you brainstorm ideas and proofread your essays but likely won't help you rewrite; some writing centers may only serve undergraduate students),

- Disability services (I would highly recommend registering for accommodations if you have a disability, including both physical and mental health conditions. This requires official documentation, so you may need to get tested in the U.S., which may or may not be covered by insurance. You can reach out to the health/counseling center to see if they offer testing or get a referral to a community provider).

These resources may have a different name and offer slightly different services at each school.

Name three resources that you plan on utilizing to support your academic success:

1 _____

_____

2 _____

_____

3 _____

_____

Tips on Studying and Engaging in the Classroom

It is important to know how to study effectively. The campus library is a valuable resource, especially if you are doing research and writing papers. The library may have designated librarians to help students from different majors, so get to know who your librarians are. One way to do this is to attend a workshop hosted by your campus library. You will develop a better understanding of how your library operates and where to find the information you need without having to figure it out all on your own. While there is usually a main campus library, some schools or departments will also have smaller libraries where the material is more specialized.

When working with international students, I often hear that there is so much assigned reading, it feels impossible to get through everything. This is where I encourage you to persevere and learn how to prioritize. An important skill is learning how to skim. Textbooks are not meant to be studied from cover to cover. Textbooks are designed with chapters that usually have objectives, content, and summary. When you study, look over the objectives and summary first, to make sure you have an idea of what you are supposed to learn from the chapter. Next, look at all the headers and quiz yourself to see if you know the concepts. For any content that you are unsure of, read more thoroughly. You can also compare your notes from class to see what was and was not covered. To be more effective, skim your textbook before class to have a sense of what will be discussed and form questions ahead of time. If reading speed is an issue, it may be useful to find the audio version of textbooks, so you can listen to the material instead. You may even be able to find educational videos on YouTube or TikTok (make sure these are reliable sources).

It is also important to have a discussion with your professor or TA to talk about study strategies. You can ask: "How can I study effectively for this class?" or "I'm having trouble getting through all of the readings, can you help me prioritize what I need to read first and what I can catch up on later?"

Depending on the class, you may need to engage with the material in particular ways. For example, if a class requires you to memorize concepts that you will be quizzed on, it might be helpful to create flashcards or find other ways to organize the information. In a discussion-based class, which may award participation points, it is important to come pre-pared with questions and comments to show that you are engaging with the material. You can write down your questions and comments while you study so that you are prepared to talk. The key to getting participation points is to speak a few times each class, so set a goal to speak once or twice. Try being the first or second student to speak, so you don't spend the whole class trying to find a good opportunity to chime in. You can even let your professor or TA know that they can call on you if you have trouble initiating. If the class is hosted online, try engaging in the discussion via the chat function or similar feature. Note that being graded on participation is classically American; being engaged is seen as a positive thing. By participating in discussions, professors can assess your understanding of the material and if you are paying attention.

For writing-intensive classes, ask your instructors or classmates for an example of a successful essay. This sample can be a helpful resource for working on your own or with the writing center. When you are learning the format of writing for these classes, it can also be helpful to ask a peer, TA, or instructor to look over a few drafts before you submit the paper. If you struggle to express yourself in English, consider writing in your native language first and then translating into English. If your syllabus and university plagiarism policies allow, you may consider utilizing tools like ChatGPT to assist you in getting started with a paper, including brainstorming ideas, structuring the essay, and correcting your grammar and spelling. It is important not to solely rely on such tools or submit the output as your own writing.

Often, students do not feel comfortable asking for accommodations because they think they are causing trouble for the professors or TAs. Reframe that thought and help them help you because your professors and TAs don't know what you need unless you tell them. Their jobs are to provide the best learning environment and to make sure that students are learning. You can ask to review the professor's slides before class and to record the lectures, so you can listen to them again. For classes on Zoom or other digital platforms, you may request closed captioning or translated captions, if they are available. Again, when in doubt, go to the professor's or TA's office hours early in the semester to ensure that you are studying effectively.

"Good Enough"

Instead of striving for unattainable perfection on every single paper, test, and presentation, it is important to consider what is "good enough." Despite what others may tell you, it is absolutely okay to prioritize other areas of your wellness! While there are minimum credit requirements for international students (typically 12 credits/semester for undergraduate and 9 credits/semester for graduate students; there may also be a limit on how many online classes can count towards the minimum), you can apply to waive that requirement, so you can take fewer classes while maintaining your visa status. It is crucial to understand what is considered a passing grade or GPA (grade point average) so that you do not jeopardize your visa status. If you are concerned about your academic performance, talk to your academic advisor or international advisor to find out what your options are (e.g., a regular or medical withdrawal from a class rather than failing it). You may be able to replace a lower grade with a higher one by retaking a class.

Declining academic performance is often a symptom rather than the root issue. Consider how things are going in the other areas of your life. If you are working 20 hours/week, stressed about finances, and don't have the time or energy to study for your midterm exams, your grades will likely suffer.

After reading this chapter, reflect:

- What are you doing well academically that you can continue to do?

- What are you struggling with academically and what do you need to do differently?

- What other things might be going on that are affecting your academic performance?

- How can you balance academics with other things in your life so that you don't jeopardize your grades or affect your visa status?

- Who can help you determine your options?

Additional Resources

The University of California-Irvine's Guide to Thrive[15] was developed for first-generation college students to gain a better understanding of common academic terminology. It's a good starting point to develop the vocabulary you need to be on the same page as faculty, staff, and administrators.

For students of color, *Letters to My Sisters and Brothers: Practical Advice to Successfully Navigate Academia as a Student of Color* by Dr. Nelson O. O. Zounlomè[16] is an engaging and one-of-a-kind workbook that utilizes culturally relevant and evidence-based activities to assist undergraduate and graduate students to move with purpose and intention during their time in higher education.

For graduate students, the *Developing a Graduate School Thrive Mindset* course[17] from Dr. Nelson O. O. Zounlomè is a great next step to help you prioritize and launch your career while in graduate school.

For graduate students who would like to have better work-life balance, another wonderful resource that many universities have adopted is the National Center for Faculty Development and Diversity (NCFDD).[18] I built my work habits using the "snack writing" method (setting aside a minimum of 30 minutes/day to engage in scholarship). From the time I was introduced to the NCFDD program to when I graduated from my doctoral program, I was able to successfully complete my written comprehensive exams and dissertation, publish 6 peer-reviewed articles (4 of them first-authored), and present 10 peer-reviewed conference posters using this method. The method also helped me complete this book in a relatively short timeframe.

---

15   http://wp.due.uci.edu/ucifirstgen/wp-content/uploads/sites/34/2016/09/SSI-Guide-to-Thrive.pdf
16   https://letterstomysistersandbrothers.com/
17   https://grad-school-thrive-mindset.thinkific.com/courses/developing-a-graduate-school-thrive-mindset
18   https://www.facultydiversity.org

Chapter 13
Investing in Your Career

This chapter includes:

- Career center support with applying for internships and connecting to alumni.

- Professional organizations that are related to your field.

To make the most of this chapter, reflect:

- What resources on and off campus are available to assist with your career planning? What services do they offer?

- What professional organizations are you currently a part of? What aspects of the professional organizations are you utilizing? What other services do they offer that you are not using?

It's never too early to start considering your career plans. Applying for internships now can help you be more competitive in the job market. Your campus career center can help. Some universities have one career center and others have college-based career centers (e.g., career services for the Business College). Career centers can provide you with guidance on putting together your resume/CV, cover letter, and applications; they also do this to help students apply for graduate school. Career centers offer a wide range of services, such as mock interviews, and give you tools to make informed decisions about your career (e.g., useful websites and assessments on interests, values, and personality). Always double-check with your Office of International Services to make sure you are within visa regulations regarding receiving course credits for the internship (the likely solution) or if you can receive payment for it. Volunteer services are another great way to boost your resume.

Name three resources to help jumpstart your career:

Example:

The School of Education Career Services, located on the 1st floor of the School of Education, can help with my resume/CV. The Center for Innovative Teaching and Learning (CITL) can review my teaching essay for faculty positions. My academic advisor can support field-specific job applications. My training director can provide information on field placements and internships.

1 _____

_____

2 _____

_____

3 _____

_____

Career centers also offer relationships with alumni. These connections are critical as 70-80% of jobs in the U.S. are never publicly listed. This means that those jobs are filled by people who have connections to those organizations, which underscores the importance of networking. Having access to a network of alumni in your field provides insider knowledge about the job market. If you did not grow up in the U.S., you may have to build your network from scratch. Ask your career center to introduce you to alumni who may be helpful to you. Once you have their contact information, reach out by introducing yourself and requesting a brief 15-20 minute phone call. These calls are an opportunity to conduct an informational interview to learn how the alumnus got to where they are in the field. Do your best to maintain contact and build relationships. This may include emailing them periodically to update them about what you're doing. This can be a lot of work; don't wait until you're about to graduate to do this!

Name three alumni you would like to contact and how they could be helpful to your career:

1 _____

_____

2 _____

_____

3 _____

_____

Lastly, consider the resources beyond your school. For example, some professional organizations have sections specifically for undergraduate/graduate students. Often, there are opportunities to be mentored by older students or professionals. I became involved with the American Psychological Association (APA) for Graduate Students (APAGS) as a master's student. Through APAGS, I connected with other students across the U.S. and attended training sessions that helped with my career. I was also introduced to different divisions of APA and found spaces specifically for international students. Later, I held leadership positions, which gave me more experience and prepared me for the job market. As an international student, it can also be helpful to look for professional organizations in your home country or other countries where you are interested in pursuing your career.

List three U.S.-based professional organizations that you can look into:

1 _____

_____

2 _____

_____

3 _____

_____

List three professional organizations in your home country/other countries that you can look into:

1 _____

_____

2 _____

_____

3 _____

_____

After reading this chapter, reflect:

- How can you best utilize the career center and off-campus resources at this stage?

- What professional organizations might you join? Where can you learn more about the professional organizations that might be a good fit for you? How can you make the most out of the professional organizations that you join?

Chapter 14
Getting Legal Advice

This chapter includes:

- Legal services and when you might need them.

To make the most of this chapter, reflect:

- Are you aware of any legal services that are available to you?

- When might you utilize legal services?

Let's face it — laws are complicated anywhere in the world. Some campuses offer legal services, so you are not left to figure the law out on your own. These services may not provide you with legal guidance on immigration (consult with the Office of International Services for immigration-related information), but they can be helpful in other ways. Legal services might include helping students draft legal documents (e.g., wills), providing legal advice (e.g., understanding a rental contract, breaking your lease), and representing you in court. For example, I was in a fender bender (a minor car accident), where the other person hit my car from behind.

The other driver's insurance company was stingy with what they offered to pay me. I was very stressed about the situation. The legal services on campus represented me and negotiated with the insurance company. Although the representative at legal services was only able to get me $100 more than the original offer, I was significantly less anxious because I didn't have to deal with the situation directly on top of my Ph.D. studies.

Name the legal services on your campus. If your campus does not have this resource, do a Google search for nearby law school clinics and/or law firms that work with students:

Example:

Student Legal Services is located in Poplars Building, 400 E. Seventh St, Room 712, Bloomington, IN 47402. They are currently accepting virtual appointments. The types of services they provide include...

_____

_____

_____

After reading this chapter, reflect:

- Based on the legal services available to you, when might you need their help? Do they offer pro bono (free) or reduced prices for students?

Chapter 15

Other Helpful On-Campus Resources

This chapter includes:

- Other on-campus resources for you to consider.

To make the most of this chapter, reflect:

- As you were doing research for the other chapters of the book, what other on-campus resources did you come across?

The resources discussed in earlier chapters are not exhaustive and different universities have different things to offer! If the school you are attending doesn't have the exact resource I mentioned, it might be called something different or exist under a different department/office. Smaller schools may not have as many resources on campus, but they may collaborate with other nearby universities or with the community (discussed in the next chapter). When in doubt, you can always ask your academic advisor, staff, colleagues, and peers.

List other on-campus resources that you have found in different domains:

Resources related to academics:

1 _____

_____

_____

2 _____

_____

_____

3 _____

_____

_____

4 _____

_____

_____

5 _____

_____

_____

Resources related to health and wellness:

1 _____

_____

_____

2 _____

_____

_____

3 _____

_____

_____

4 _____

_____

_____

5 _____

_____

_____

Resources related to social activities:

1 _____

_____

_____

2 _____

_____

_____

3 _____

_____

_____

4 _____

_____

_____

5 _____

_____

_____

Resources related to _____:

1 _____

_____

_____

2 _____

_____

_____

3 _____

_____

_____

4 _____

_____

_____

5 _____

_____

_____

Resources related to _____:

1 _____

_____

_____

2 _____

_____

_____

3 _____

_____

_____

4 _____

_____

_____

5 _____

_____

_____

After reading this chapter, reflect:

- Look at the list you created and consider when you might utilize these on-campus resources.

Chapter 16

Familiarizing Yourself with Local and Community Resources

This chapter includes:

- Local library resources and apps.

- Women's shelters.

- Food banks, food pantries, or soup kitchens.

- Urgent care and emergency rooms.

To make the most of this chapter, reflect:

- What neighborhood or county do you currently reside in?

- What local in-person and online communities are you a part of?

It may seem like there are so many on-campus resources that learning about community resources is overdoing it. Here's the thing, when you are under stress or in crisis, the first reaction is not to look up resources, it's usually panic or feeling stuck. It's important to be aware of what is around you so that it is easier to access support – for you or a friend in need. Community resources may also be cheaper, more convenient, comprehensive, and provide greater privacy to those who access them.

One way to identify local resources is to use a search engine to look up "[neighborhood/county name] + resources."

Local Library, Libby, and Hoopla

When it comes to the local library, people usually think of borrowing books and DVDs. In my opinion, the local library is vastly underappreciated given how many resources may be hosted there. For example, many local libraries serve as career centers, reviewing resumes and cover letters as well as practicing mock interviews. They also provide a broad range of free workshops and family-friendly events. Once you have a local address, bring your ID and lease (or a utility bill with your name and address) to the library to get a free library card. Many libraries in the U.S. also use free apps, like Libby or Hoopla, so you can easily check out e-books and audiobooks. I have read so many more books using the apps.

Where is your local library, what are its hours of operation, and what additional services does it provide:

_____

_____

_____

_____

_____

_____

Women's Shelter

For women international students (with or without children), this is a resource that is helpful to know about. If you are experiencing physical, psychological, or emotional abuse from an intimate partner (also known as domestic abuse), you may want to consider this resource. Many women's shelters provide other services, such as a 24-hour hotline, legal advocacy, medical aid, counseling, and support groups. Typically, for the safety of the people they serve, shelter addresses are not publicly available, so it is best to call. Some women's shelters are more gender-inclusive, accepting cis women (people who were assigned female at birth and are women), trans women (people who were assigned male at birth and are women), and non-binary folks (people who identify outside of the woman/man binary).

Note the phone number and website for the local women's shelter:

_____

_____

_____

_____

Food Bank, Food Pantry, or Soup Kitchen

During the COVID-19 pandemic, across 800 campuses in the U.S., approximately 52% of college students utilized food banks and 30% used them more than once. Some universities have food pantries for their students to donate to and/or utilize. If your school does not have such a resource, you may want to be aware of resources in the broader community. You may also want to research who is eligible to access these resources. Some food banks might require a referral from a professional.

Identify the location of your local food bank, food pantry, or soup kitchen, their hours, and eligibility requirement to utilize their services:

_____

_____

_____

_____

Urgent Care and Emergency Room

Whether you are experiencing a physical or mental health crisis, it is important to know where to access these resources. In some locations, in addition to hospital emergency rooms (ERs), there are urgent care facilities. ERs treat life-threatening health conditions while urgent care centers are the middle ground between your primary care provider and the ER. Providers at an urgent care center can help determine if they can meet your needs on-site or if you need to access an ER or other support. ER visits can be quite costly, depending on your health insurance. For this reason, if their health allows, many people drive, get a ride, or use a ride-sharing service to get to the ER, rather than using an ambulance. If you are in a larger urban area, you may have access to multiple providers. Be sure to do your research ahead of time to know where you can access better care.

Where are the closest urgent care centers and emergency rooms:

_____

_____

_____

_____

After reading this chapter, reflect:

- How can you keep this information on hand in a way that is useful to you?

- What other community resources did you uncover while doing research? Add them to your list!

Chapter 17

Putting It All Together and Next Steps

This chapter includes:

- Familiarizing yourself with the various resources you listed.

To make the most of this chapter, reflect:

- What forms of transportation are available for you to get around campus or the community?

- How are you being supported as an international student by individuals, programs, departments, schools/colleges, and the university?

- How can individuals, programs, departments, schools/ colleges, and the university better support you?

Congratulations! You have done a lot of work to become familiar with the resources on and off campus. I know it can be overwhelming to sort through so much information. I want to invite you to pause and take a few deep breaths.

As you get to know your campus and community, take yourself on a tour to visit these spaces, or even just to walk or drive by. You can organize these visits by location or by category. For example, if the Career Center and the Health Center are located on the north side of campus, then visiting them together makes a lot of sense. Or you could do a tour to visit all the resources that are under the category of career achievement (e.g., Career Center, libraries). These tours can be great study breaks and provide a way to connect with others who are interested in becoming more familiar with the campus.

After reading this chapter, reflect:

- Make a plan to visit these resources: When and how will you go?

The next section is advice for staff and faculty who work with international students. Consider reading through it and reflecting on how you can advocate with staff and faculty to build support for yourself and your international peers. Otherwise, you can skip ahead to the closing and additional resources section. All of the additional resources referenced throughout the sections are organized at the end of the book. Be sure to check them out!

Advice for Staff and Faculty on Supporting International Students

Hello faculty and staff! Thank you for picking up this book. While this book was written for international students, in this section, I focus on the ways you can better support international students in your capacity as a staff or faculty member.

In this section of the book, I address the following:

- What faculty and staff can do before international students arrive on campus.

- How faculty and staff can better work with international students.

- Supporting international students in the classroom.

- Supporting international students on campus.

- Information on how CIP codes impact international students and how to change your program's CIP code, if relevant.

- Additional resources on international student adjustment and cross-cultural communication.

To make the most of this chapter, reflect:

- How are you already supporting international students as individuals and/or on the programmatic, departmental, school/college, and university levels? How are those initiatives going?

- How can you better support international students as individuals and/or on the programmatic, departmental, school/college, and university levels?

- What are the rewards and challenges when working with international students in your role?

General Advice

Recruiting a diverse student body is something to be proud of but it is also critical to consider ways to support and retain diversity (including historically marginalized and international students). Whether you have one or many international students in your program, department, or school, you should consider educating yourself on immigration issues and the unique needs of international students. I also recommend building a relationship with the Office of International Services and familiarizing yourself with on-and off-campus resources.

When I was applying to doctoral programs, others recommended working with faculty members with international backgrounds because they were more likely (a) to have an interest in what I wanted to study, which was mental health among the international student population, and (b) to understand and advocate for the unique experiences and needs of an international student advisee. While personal experience is useful, it would also be helpful for domestic faculty to be equipped to work with and advise international students.

As a busy faculty member myself, I know that being asked to do more can be overwhelming. You don't need to know the ins and outs of immigration policy, but it helps to know the basics and to be able to point students to further resources. The tips I provide below aren't just beneficial for international students but can also support inclusivity for students of various identities and backgrounds.

Consider reaching out to international students before they arrive on campus. I know from personal experience that having connections with faculty and staff prior to coming to the U.S. made a huge difference. Knowing at least one person I could reach out to in a foreign place was comforting and made the journey less daunting. Reach out to the international students you work with to establish a more personal connection. If you cannot meet in person before school starts, send them a personalized email or schedule a video call to say hi and welcome them. When they arrive on campus, get to know them individually by asking about how they view their culture and the similarities/differences they have observed in their time in the U.S. (e.g., "Can you tell me more about your culture? What are some similarities or differences you've observed so far?"). This will challenge you to move beyond assumptions or stereotypes, support the student to develop more awareness around barriers to adjustment, and create a foundation so students will feel more comfortable reaching out for help down the line.

Building a relationship with the Office of International Services can facilitate collaboration with international advisors to help international students succeed in school and their future careers. Some ways to build this relationship include learning about how international student advising works and introducing yourself to the designated advisors. Later on, you might help advocate for your students by attending some of their meetings with them.

Lastly, you can also work through this book with your international student(s). If you do not know all the resources that are available to them, you can assign your student to look up relevant on- and off-campus resources, report back to you, and discuss how such resources can be utilized.

Supporting International Students in the Classroom

In *Chapter 12: Thriving in Academics*, I share tips for students. Here, I'll share how you, as a faculty member, can support international students in your classroom.

In the second semester of my master's program, I had a course where I submitted ten reflection papers. I received points off of all ten papers because my formatting was incorrect. After I submitted my last reflection paper, my professor finally shared this feedback — implying that I was trying to get away with using bigger spacing so that I did not have to write as much. I was embarrassed and, honestly, quite angry. My professor could have given me this feedback after I submitted my first reflection, but he chose to share it at the end. I tried to set up a meeting, but he didn't respond until after he submitted the final grades for the class. Needless to say, I wasn't happy with my grade or my experience with him. I went to my advisor, who also identified as Taiwanese international, to figure out what the comment meant. My advisor and I discovered that my version of Microsoft Word was set up for Chinese writing, with bigger default spacing than the English setting; we resolved the formatting with the click of a button. Even something as small as formatting can have cross-cultural implications and misunderstandings. I wish I had had an earlier opportunity to address the formatting issue with my professor. It's best to communicate expectations and concerns clearly, early, and often – before something small turns into something bigger.

Classroom culture and expectations, which can differ based on the professor who is teaching the course, may be completely different from what international students are accustomed to. I encourage you to consider all the factors that make a student successful, including navigating online learning platforms, understanding the syllabus, utilizing office hours, participating in class discussions, completing assignments, passing exams, and avoiding plagiarism. The best thing to do is to spell out your expectations, goals, and objectives so they are clear. For example, if your final grades include participation points, it might be helpful to say "Everyone is expected to speak up at least once per class. It's fine to circle back to prior topics if you still want to discuss something about those topics. If I notice that you've been quiet for a while, I may call on you. You are allowed to ask me to come back to you later if you are still gathering your thoughts." Consider normalizing reading from notes, rather than speaking extemporaneously; it may take a bit of courage for some to speak up in class, especially for English-language-learners. If students are joining via Zoom, allow them to participate in class discussions via chat. Another useful tool for setting expectations is to provide examples of what a successful essay or assignment would look like and why it is considered exemplary.

Students whose first language is not English may be more fluent in reading and writing than in conversation. It may be useful to them if you can provide a visual aid like slides or handouts; even referring to the text of the reading materials may help them to follow along. If you do have such materials, consider sharing them prior to the class so students have a chance to review them ahead of time. Allowing students to record lectures so they can re-listen to them can also help with comprehension. If using Zoom or a similar service, turn on closed captioning or translated captions whenever possible. It can be helpful to check with students about the accuracy of the translated captions and determine which one to use.[19]

Remind students to utilize additional campus resources, such as the writing center, library, and tutoring services when they are working on their assignments. Consider requiring students to visit these centers and offices. Completing their drafts early for their appointments will help them plan ahead so that they receive the full benefits of the services.

Finally, given the ubiquity of tools such as ChatGPT, it may be useful to teach students how to utilize them effectively rather than relying on such tools (e.g., how to expand upon ideas from the information that ChatGPT provides rather than just submitting the output as their own work).

Supporting International Students on Campus

Student Events — One way for people with different social identities and cultural backgrounds to challenge their misconceptions of each other is to increase their exposure to and social connectedness with one another. Planning intercultural events for international students and domestic students can support this goal. I recommend having the first half of the event be more structured to help break the ice. For example, having everyone introduce themselves in a speed dating-like format allows them to talk to different people. It can be helpful to

---

19   Scroll halfway down the webpage to see the average length of time for students to achieve proficiency in English: https://www.state.gov/foreign-language-training/

provide information on appropriate ways to ask about someone's culture (e.g., "Tell me about some of the traditions in your culture and how you practice them." "What are some things that your culture values and how do you view those values?"). It can also be a useful opportunity to educate attendees about the etiquette of social events in the U.S. (e.g., what is small talk, small talk topics). For the second half of the event, having less structure allows folks to practice what they just learned, mingle, and have deeper and more meaningful conversations.

Phone and Virtual Services — For staff who offer phone and virtual assistance, such as front desk staff and librarians, consider adding a visual and/or chat component to your support to make your assistance more accessible. Many international (and domestic) students are nervous on the phone due to language issues, social anxiety, etc. This is one of the most common reasons students do not schedule with the counseling center. Another solution is to offer online scheduling.

Counseling Centers — For mental health clinicians, if your counseling center does not currently offer an international student support group, consider starting one. Given the unique experiences of international students, it can be helpful to have a confidential space dedicated to them where they can support one another and build social connections. Consider if the group meeting time would accommodate students who may also be parents. Participants from one of the groups that I co-facilitated shared how seeing other international folks in a counseling group normalized help-seeking behaviors, so they did not feel like the only ones with difficulties and concerns. Support groups are also a great opportunity to provide education about mental health services and break down stigma about seeking mental health care.

When hiring new staff and clinicians, the search committee can prioritize recruiting clinicians with identities that match the demographics of the student population, including nationality and languages spoken. It is crucial that the clinician is not just proficient in the language but also utilizes evidence-based best practices and has the competency to provide care in that language, such as knowing how symptoms of mental health may present in various populations. For example, Chinese international students experiencing depression often report feelings of numbness rather than sadness. Another way to increase cultural sensitivity when working with international students is to identify experts (especially if there is no one on staff) who can provide consultation services or co-facilitate case conferences for staff. Such experts can be professors who study international student concerns and/or mental health providers from other counseling centers or in the community who have a specialty in working with the relevant population. It is also helpful to build relationships with clinicians in the community who you can refer international students to. It is worth noting that not all international students prefer to see a clinician who speaks their native language; some students may appreciate the cultural and psychological distance that speaking English provides.

CIP Code

I **highly** encourage departments and programs to look into how their programs are coded (termed CIP code) by the Department of Homeland Security (DHS). While the coding may not matter for domestic students, it can have a significant impact on international students after they graduate. If a department reports its program as STEM (science, technology, engineering, and math), international students who graduate from those programs can extend their optional practical training (OPT) up to three years. An international student from a non-STEM program can only stay one year. One reason some fields have fewer international students is that these fields (e.g., counseling, education, nursing) need clinical/practice hours post-graduation to meet the requirements for certification or licensure; if international students can only stay one year after graduation, it makes it difficult to meet those requirements.

Being listed as a STEM program can also help you to be viewed as being more competitive, which can help draw top students from around the world. In turn, your international students would have more choice and autonomy regarding where they go after graduation.

To learn more about CIP codes and what qualifies a program to be considered STEM, see the links below:

https://studyinthestates.dhs.gov/stem-opt-hub/additional-resources/eligible-cip-codes-for-the-stem-opt-extension

https://www.ice.gov/sites/default/files/documents/stem-list.pdf

https://nces.ed.gov/ipeds/cipcode/Default.aspx?y=56

Learning more about the requirements can help you to identify if this is an option for your program. For example, some business programs were able to list themselves as STEM by adding additional statistics courses into their curriculum. For an international student, that could make all the difference.

If your program requires post-graduation clinical/placement hours to get licensure or certification but does not qualify as a STEM program, lay the information out clearly on your department/program's website so international students are aware of how their status can impact their career prospects. As academics, we can do a better job of being transparent and showing care for students beyond their time in our programs.

The advice given in this chapter is not meant to be comprehensive but to start a conversation among staff and faculty to identify gaps in knowledge, what tools are needed, and to plan to better serve the international student population on campus.

After reading this section, reflect:

- What ideas or recommendations can you apply to your work with international students as individuals and/or on the programmatic, departmental, schools/colleges, and university levels?

- What other resources do you need to work more effectively with international students?

Additional Resources

Here are some meta-analyses in the international student literature that may help contextualize some of the issues this population faces:

Bender, M., van Osch, Y., Sleegers, W., & Ye, M. (2019). Social support benefits psychological adjustment of international students: *Evidence from a meta-analysis. Journal of Cross-Cultural Psychology, 50*(7), 827-847.

Zhang, J., & Goodson, P. (2011). Predictors of international students' psychosocial adjustment to life in the United States: A systematic review. *International Journal of Intercultural Relations, 35*(2),139–162.

You may be able to find research articles on ways to better support your international students. For example, here is an excellent article on providing culturally relevant services for international Black African students:

Onyenekwu, I. U. (2017). Providing culturally relevant services for international Black African collegians in the United States: A guide for student affairs professionals. *Journal of International Students, 7*(4), 1113-1125.

Here is an article that goes beyond social support and discusses organizational support:

Cho, J., & Yu, H. (2015). Roles of university support for international students in the United States: Analysis of a systematic model of university identification, university support, and psychological well-being. *Journal of Studies in International Education, 19*(1), 11–27.

Here is an excellent podcast that discusses cross-cultural communication and how it might show up in the classroom and teamwork:

Armchair Expert with Dax Shepard—Erin Meyer (https://open.spotify. com/episode/5R9vPmkDFBi4iWaEY7fMS6?si= KqeBowrrSNKZCNCgcKXl9w)

Closing

Dear You,

Congratulations on making it to the end of the book!

In addition to hard work, my success is built upon the support and assistance I received from others. Writing this book was humbling because it allowed me to take stock of the people and resources I had and continue to have access to. Even now, as a faculty member, I am constantly struck by the kindness and generosity of others and by the time and attention they provide so I can continue to learn and grow.

In turn, my hope is that this guide helps you become resourceful. By building a database of resources, you can save time and invest energy in different areas of your life. I encourage you to revisit different sections of the book in various stages of your academic journey as your needs shift and the type of help you require changes. While you may not utilize all the resources available to you, I hope you find it empowering to know where to seek help if you need it.

Lastly, I hope that this book gives you the opportunity to practice your thriving skills and become savvy at navigating different environments, wherever you go in the future.

I wish you the best of luck in your future endeavors!

Warmly,

Lei Wang, Ph.D.

Acknowledgments

When I was little, my dream was to become a published author. While I have already published several academic articles, I had given up on the idea of creating content for the layperson. I would like to acknowledge the folks behind the scenes who helped make this publication a reality.

First, I would like to thank God for guiding me on my journey and for providing me with the strength, inspiration, and persistence to complete this book. I would like to offer my appreciation and gratitude to my partner and publisher, and the Founder and CEO of Liberate The Block, Dr. Nelson O. O. Zounlomè for his consistent encouragement and feedback throughout the process. Without him paving the way, it is very unlikely I would have considered sharing my work this way.

Thanks to Ms. Carrier Fleider and Drs. Brian TaeHyuk Keum, Jeeseon Park-Saltzman, Kenneth T. Wang, Koyun 'Alice' Chi, Maureen Chinwendu Onyeziri, Shu-Yi Wang, and Yu Chak Sunny Ho for providing feedback during the early stages of this process and for playing important roles during my graduate school journey.

I would also like to express gratitude towards my friend and illustrator, Dr. Shao-Jung 'Stella' Ko who did a splendid job with the artwork and offered suggestions to improve iTHRIVE. I appreciate Dr. Nelson O. O. Zounlomè (editor) and the Kaleidoscope Vibrations, LLC team: Katherine Kolios (editor) for the thoughtful feedback to make this book so much better, Caroline Rinaldy (formatter) for transforming iTHRIVE from a Word document to an actual book, and the reviewers, Dr. Shaznin Daruwalla, Dr. Bongjoo Hwang, Ashna Sangar, and Rojina Regmi who offered their kind words and helpful feedback.

Because of the abundant support I received, I wholeheartedly believe that iTHRIVE can make the impact I want on my readers — offering tips and providing mentorship to international students so they can better their lives and THRIVE while studying abroad.

References and Additional Resources

Visit www.iTHRIVEbook.com to access downloadable worksheets and links to resources!

Getting Started

Chapter 1: Why do I want to study in the U.S.?

- Reasons why everyone wants to study in the U.S.: https://www.mastersportal.com/articles/839/5-reasons-why-everyone-wants-to-study-in-the-us.html

- 7 Reasons why students think U.S.A. is the holy grail of higher education: https://www.mastersportal.com/articles/1216/7-reasons-why-students-think-usa-is-the-holy-grail-of-higher-education.html

- Open Doors Data from the Institute of International Education: https://opendoorsdata.org/

Chapter 2: Now that I've decided that I want to pursue an education in the U.S., what's next?

- U.S. News Rankings: https://www.usnews.com/best-colleges

- LinkedIn: https://www.linkedin.com/

- Open Doors Data from the Institute of International Education: https://opendoorsdata.org/

Chapter 3: Help! What do I do with the applications and interviews?

- University of Missouri Career Center on writing a resume: https://career.missouri.edu/resumes-cover-letters/writing-a-resume/

Chapter 5: Planning Ahead: Connecting with current students, securing housing, purchasing textbooks, and making travel plans

Securing Housing

- https://www.craigslist.org

- https://www.apartment.com

~~Surviving~~ Thriving in the U.S.

Chapter 8: Homesickness, psychological adjustment, and facing discrimination

Homesickness

- Wang, K. T., Wei, M., Zhao, R., Chuang, C. C., & Li, F. (2015). The Cross-Cultural Loss Scale: Development and psychometric evaluation. *Psychological Assessment, 27*(1), 42-53. https://doi.org/10.1037/pas0000027

Psychological Adjustment and Identity Shifts

- Schartner, A., & Young, T. J. (2016) Towards an integrated conceptual model of international student adjustment and adaptation. *European Journal of Higher Education, 6*(4), 372-386. https://doi.org/10.1080/21568235.2016.1201775

- Berry, J. W. (1994). Acculturation and psychological adaptation. In A.-M. Bouvy, F. J. R. van de Vijver, P. Boski, & P. Schmitz (Eds.), *Journeys into Cross Cultural Psychology* (pp. 129–141). Swets & Zeitlinger.

- Fries-Britt, S., Mwangi, C. A. G., & Peralta, A. M. (2014). Learning race in a U.S. context: An emergent framework on the perceptions of race among foreign-born students. *Journal of Diversity in Higher Education, 7*(1), 1–13. https://doi.org/10.1037/a0035636

Discrimination and Stereotypes

- Walton, J., & Truong, M. (2023). A review of the model minority myth: Understanding the social, educational and health impacts. *Ethnic & Racial Studies, 46*(3), 391-419. https://doi.org/10.1080/01419870.2022.2121170

- Ukpokodu, O. N. (2018). African immigrants, the "New Model Minority": Examining the reality in US K-12 schools. *The Urban Review, 50*, 69-96. https://doi.org/10.1007/s11256-017-0430-0

Chapter 9: Attending to your physical, mental, and spiritual health

Mental and Emotional Health

- National Suicide Prevention and Crisis Lifeline: 988 and https://suicidepreventionlifeline.org

Chapter 11: Taking care of your financial well-being

H1B Visa and Green Card

- https://h1bgrader.com/

Additional Resources

- *Get Good with Money* written by Tiffany "the Budgetnista" Aliche

Chapter 12: Thriving in academics

- *The Guide to Thrive*: http://wp.due.uci.edu/ucifirstgen/wp-content/uploads/sites/34/2016/09/SSI-Guide-to-Thrive.pdf

- *Letters to My Sisters and Brothers: Practical Advice to Successfully Navigate Academia as a Student of Color* by Dr. Nelson O. O. Zounlomè: https://letterstomysistersandbrothers.com/

- *Developing a Graduate School Thrive Mindset* course: https://grad-school-thrive-mindset.thinkific.com/courses/developing-a-graduate-school-thrive-mindset

- National Center for Faculty Development and Diversity: https://www.facultydiversity.org

Advice for Staff and Faculty on Supporting International Students

Supporting International Students in the Classroom

- https://www.state.gov/foreign-language-training

CIP Code

- https://studyinthestates.dhs.gov/stem-opt-hub/additional-resources/eligible-cip-codes-for-the-stem-opt-extension

- https://www.ice.gov/sites/default/files/documents/stem-list.pdf

- https://nces.ed.gov/ipeds/cipcode/Default.aspx?y=56

Additional Resources

- Bender, M., van Osch, Y., Sleegers, W., & Ye, M. (2019). Social support benefits psychological adjustment of international students: Evidence from a meta-analysis. *Journal of Cross-Cultural Psychology, 50*(7), 827-847. https://doi.org/10.1177/0022022119861151

- Zhang, J., & Goodson, P. (2011). Predictors of international students' psychosocial adjustment to life in the United States: A systematic review. *International Journal of Intercultural Relations, 35*(2),139–162. https://doi.org/10.1016/j.ijintrel.2010.11.011

- Onyenekwu, I. U. (2017). Providing culturally relevant services for international Black African collegians in the United States: A guide for student affairs professionals. *Journal of International Students, 7*(4), 1113-1125. https://doi.org/10.5281/zenodo.1035975

- Cho, J., & Yu, H. (2015). Roles of university support for international students in the United States: Analysis of a systematic model of university identification, university support, and psychological well-being. *Journal of Studies in International Education, 19*(1), 11–27. https://doi.org/10.1177/1028315314533606

- Armchair Expert with Dax Shepard—Erin Meyer (https://open.spotify.com/episode/5R9vPmkDFBi4iWaEY7fMS6?si=Uq6zYqCUSfGeZoVt3aSyiA)